Palmistry

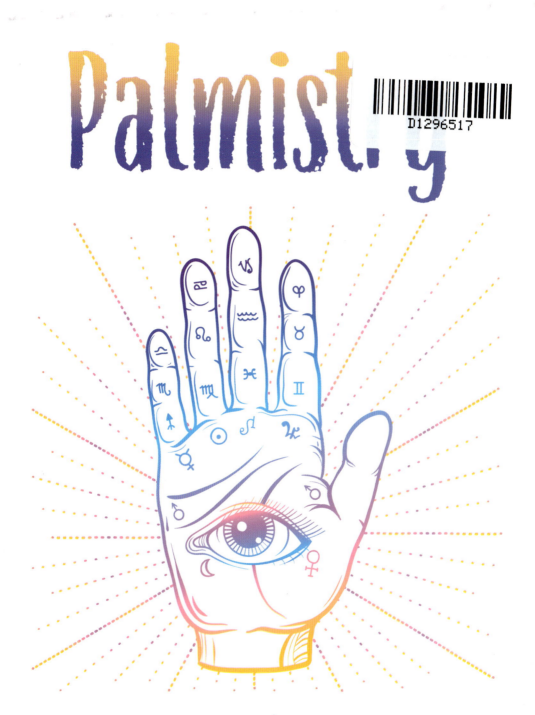

Publications International, Ltd.

Contributing writer: Lisa Brooks

Images: Shutterstock.com

Louis Weber, CEO
Publications International, Ltd.
8140 Lehigh Avenue
Morton Grove, IL 60053

ISBN: 978-1-64030-647-9

Manufactured in China.

8 7 6 5 4 3 2 1

TABLE OF CONTENTS

ISN'T IT CHIROMANTIC?

Palmistry, or **CHIROMANCY**, is one of the oldest forms of western divination. Enough people were practicing palm reading in Greece in the 300s B.C. that Alexander the Great asked Aristotle for his take, and the Aristotelian text forms the first body of knowledge about western palmistry.

THE WORD CHIROMANCY COMES FROM GREEK KHEIR-, MEANING HAND, AND -MANTEIA, MEANING DIVINATION.

Palm readers look at the human hand and look at specific lines, areas, patterns of wear, and other markers that correspond with qualities about our lives.

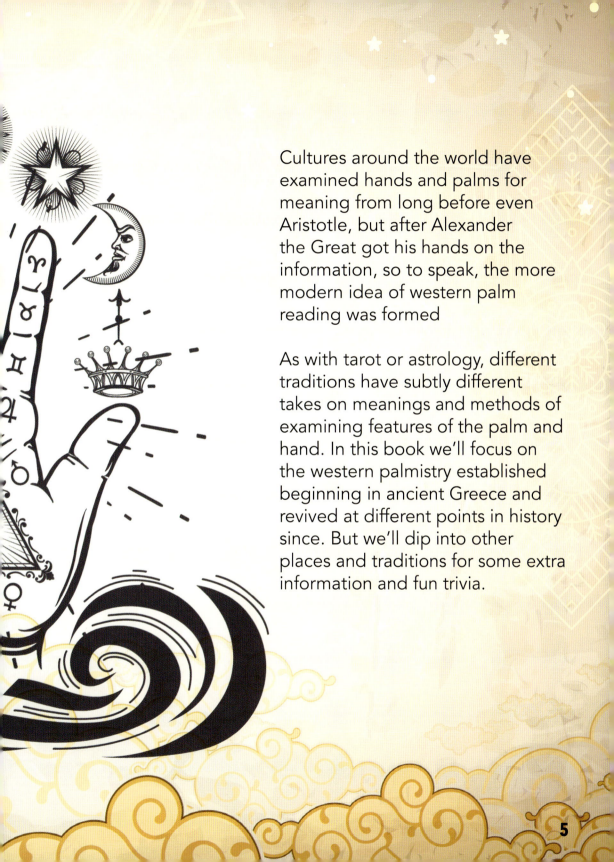

Cultures around the world have examined hands and palms for meaning from long before even Aristotle, but after Alexander the Great got his hands on the information, so to speak, the more modern idea of western palm reading was formed

As with tarot or astrology, different traditions have subtly different takes on meanings and methods of examining features of the palm and hand. In this book we'll focus on the western palmistry established beginning in ancient Greece and revived at different points in history since. But we'll dip into other places and traditions for some extra information and fun trivia.

HANDS-ON-ARISTOTLE

Hands are often our most direct form of contact with the world, used daily to work, greet others, communicate our feelings, and interact with countless objects. Some workers are even simply called hands, like farmhands or deckhands. We may bite our fingernails or pick at our cuticles out of stress, or clench our fists when we feel enraged. We use our hands to hide our eyes or cover our mouths, to hold our noses when we jump into the water, and to reach out when we lose our balance.

"This fin has four regular bone-fingers, the index, middle, ring, and little finger. But all these are permanently lodged in their fleshy covering, as the human fingers in an artificial covering. 'However recklessly the whale may sometimes serve us,' said humorous Stubb one day, 'he can never be truly said to handle us without mittens.'"
— *Herman Melville*

Why are hands so demonstrative of our character and lifestyle? For those with able bodies, our hands are graceful and gifted, able to learn tasks and repeat them easily and automatically. Our fingertips are packed with nerve endings that read very subtle sensational cues and help us navigate safely in the world, but also bring us great joy when we pet a soft animal or ruffle the bristles of a toothbrush. So much of our lives is lived through our hands.

Our hands look symmetrical at a glance, but like any twinned body feature, they really aren't the same. The dominant hand tends to be slightly larger with slightly thicker fingers and more wear because it's used so much more often.

CHIROGNOMISTS, FROM GREEK KHEIR-, MEANING HAND, AND -GNOMON, MEANING EXAMINER, HAVE IDENTIFIED AND NAMED DIFFERENT PARTS OF THE HAND,

which we'll use in this book to help you find features and read their significance. Like numerology, tarot, or other forms of divination, palmistry doesn't rely on any kind of psychic phenomena. You only need some time and dedication and to keep an open mind as you study the hand.

Scholars and advocates of palmistry have done the hard work for you over millennia of study and observation.

MOST IMPORTANTLY

Palmistry is serious for many people. This book is a fun beginner's guide to one kind of palm reading, intended to give you tools to look closely and speculate with your friends and other loved ones. "Thinking is hard," the philosopher Daniel Dennett wrote. "Thinking about some problems is so hard it can make your head ache just thinking about thinking about them." It boggles our minds to consider our futures, whether our choices make sense and are good for us, and how we can live better lives today. Practicing palmistry can help you bring these questions into focus.

In the year 1550, Michel de Nostradame, a French physician and astronomer better known as Nostradamus, published his famous work *The Prophecies*. Over the centuries, Nostradamus has been credited for predicting everything from the French Revolution to the Apollo moon landing to the September 11 terrorist attacks. While experts (and armchair experts) have often criticized the possible-prophet's writings as nothing more than vague metaphors that can be interpreted a myriad of different ways, Nostradamus remains one of the most famous—if not the most famous—fortune-tellers in history. He was certainly a favorite among internet chain-letter writers and, today, the Facebook meme crowd.

But the origins of predicting the future go back much further than the time of Nostradamus, with practitioners employing dozens of different methods for divining information about the future: numerology, reading tea leaves, astrology, tarot cards, dream predictions, and gazing into crystal balls, just to name a few.

Divination dates back at least to ancient times and probably much further. The oldest cave paintings in the world show people dancing and doing other social rituals where people might have wanted certain outcomes like calmer weather or better luck with hunting. Many ancient religions focused on interpreting signs from whimsical and moody gods, and even Christian beliefs about God's judgment or response to prayer can be seen as trying to hear predictable feedback.

SOME METHODS, SUCH AS HARUSPICY—READING THE LIVERS OF SACRIFICED ANIMALS— OR ALECTRYOMANCY— PREDICTIONS MADE BY ROOSTERS PECKING AT GRAIN—

have not seen much mainstream success in countries like the United States. But reading tea leaves or coffee grounds is so popular around the world that there are mass-produced tea sets and other aids to reading these leafy leavings, including many in English.

WHAT IS DIVINATION?

Along with tarot, there is one fortune-telling method that is quite familiar, its adherents practicing in strip malls and tidy homes and making appearances at parties. Words are not even necessary to recognize the location of a practitioner—merely a sign featuring an open hand.

This recognizable symbol, of course, indicates the practice of "chiromancy," better known as palm reading.

Although the precise origins of palmistry are unknown, the practice has been around since ancient times, most likely beginning in India. Early Hindu texts describe the palms as a way to understand ourselves and our relationships with others: a blueprint, if you will, of each individual's human experience.

And the ancient Hindu poet Valmiki, who is thought to have written one of the first epic

poems in history, the *Ramayana*, is also credited with writing a text called *The Teachings of Valmiki Maharshi on Male Palmistry* several thousand years ago.

From India, the practice spread to China, Egypt, Persia, Greece, and into Europe. Even Julius Caesar and Alexander the Great took an interest in palmistry, turning to helpers like Aristotle and analyzing the lines on their own hands and those of their officers.

Much like finding the wind or looking at the sky for auspicious signs, leaders viewed this as just one more data point that might help them win battles and protect lives.

But why hands? What has made these unassuming body parts such a source of fascination throughout time and place? As it turns out, there's a lot more to our hands than most of us realize, and in the rest of this book we'll explore just how special our hands are.

Temple of Palmistry, A-Y-P, Seattle, 1909

ABOUT HANDS

We don't spend much time thinking about our hands, but they're amazing body parts. With 27 bones, 29 joints, 17 muscles, and 123 ligaments, they are much more complex than it would seem at first glance. Our opposable thumbs set us apart from other animals, and our fingerprints—which are completely unique for every individual—set us apart from other human beings.

Our hands can tell a story about what kind of life we live: callused hands may suggest a career in construction, plumbing, or carpentry; or musicians may have calluses from playing guitars, the thumbhook on a clarinet, or how they hold drumsticks. Children and adults who write by hand a lot have calluses where the pen or pencil rests on their fingers. The hands of doctors or parents or chefs may be dry and cracked from frequent washing, while office workers or homebodies may be able to keep their hands soft and unmarred.

Someone going through a period of great stress might absentmindedly chew on their fingernails, resulting in ragged tips and cuticles; and athletes like boxers, wrestlers, and football players often have hand injuries to nurse back to health. Traumas can cause fingernails to fall off, temporarily or forever. And while movies greatly exaggerate how well you can remove your fingerprints, some kinds of chemotherapy can temporarily remove them. (What fictional criminals don't seem to realize is how scarred or burned fingerprints just become a new unique way to identify them.)

CHyromancy,

Also, the tope of the longe finger Zenith East
the wrest Nader West, the thombe side North,
and the other South, as here followeth.

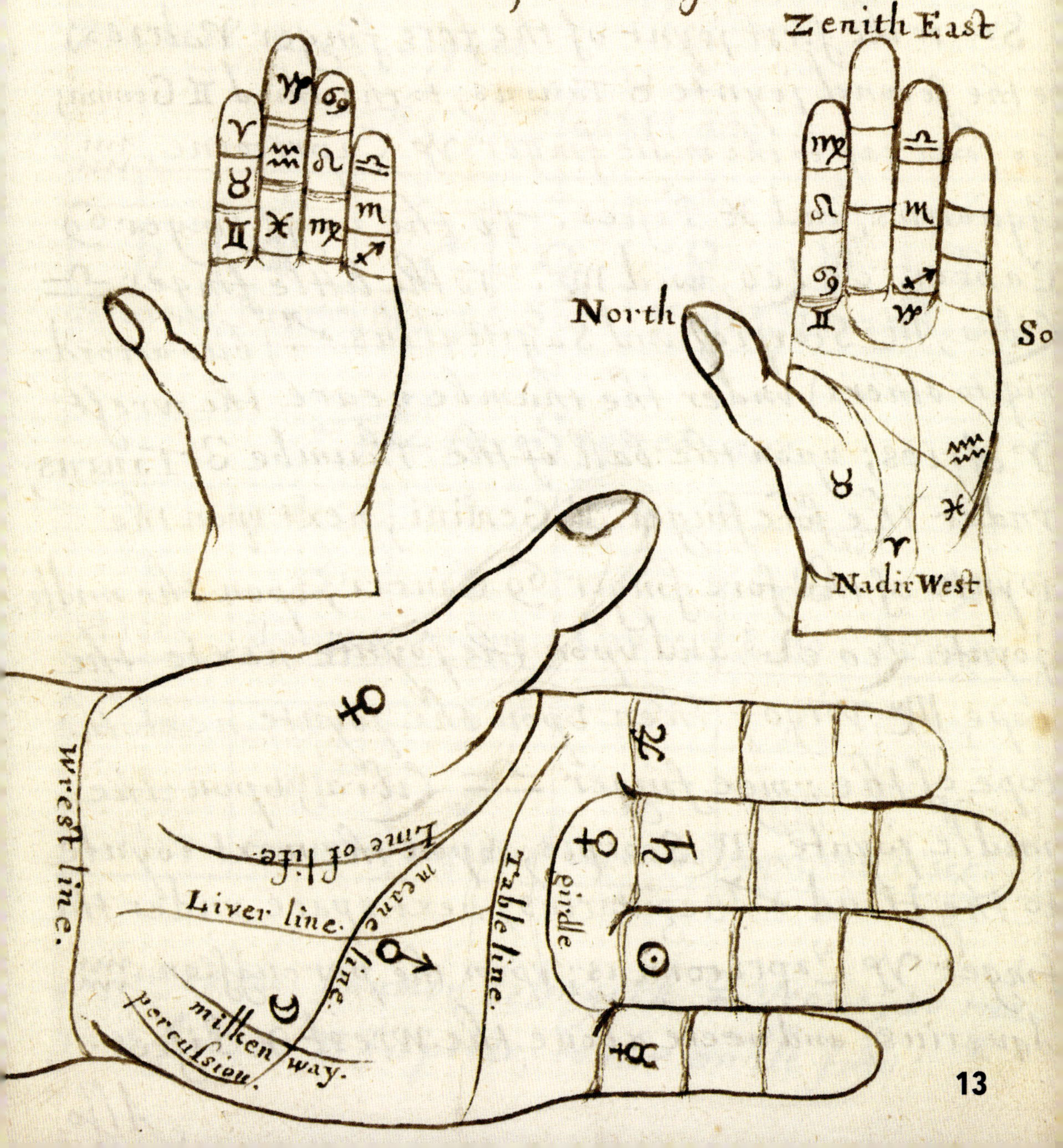

Zenith East

North

So

Nadir West

wrest line.

Line of life.

Meane line.

Liver line.

Table line.

girdle

milken way.

percussion.

13

ABOUT HANDS

"Living much out of doors, in the sun and wind, will no doubt produce a certain roughness of character—will cause a thicker cuticle to grow over some of the finer qualities of our nature, as on the face and hands, or as severe manual labor robs the hands of some of their delicacy of touch."
—Henry David Thoreau

Clearly, hands can hold a lifetime of information, telling a different story for each individual person. And history and folklore seem to support the idea that hands have been valued or sometimes even revered as powerful symbols in cultures around the world. The occurrence of hand symbols in human history goes back at least tens of thousands of years. IN FACT, THE FIRST INSTANCES OF HANDS IN ART FORM WERE FOUND IN 40,000-YEAR-OLD CAVE DRAWINGS IN INDONESIA, SPAIN, AND FRANCE.

Many more hand paintings have been found around the world, dating back thousands of years, everywhere from Australia to the United States. Created by adults and children alike, these hand drawings were formed in several different ways: An artist could place their hand on rock and then blow paint or charcoal powder from either their mouth or through a reed, making a stencil; they could paint around the outline of the hand with a brush; or they could paint their entire hand, then press it to the rock, leaving an impression. Your Thanksgiving handprint turkey has a stately ancestry.

ABOUT HANDS

The meaning of these primitive hand symbols is unclear. Since the hands have often been found near drawings of other objects, such as animals, human shapes, and geometric shapes, perhaps they were a way for the artist to "sign" their work. Or they may have been part of religious or spiritual rituals. Since most of the hand drawings have been found in caves, archeologists believe that caves may have been considered doorways to a supernatural world, and the hand prints were considered a way of drawing supernatural energy from the rock. Some hand drawings have been found with spiral shapes drawn into the palms, giving the suggestion of energy emanating from the open hand.

Later, people realized handprints were identifiable enough that they could be used as a signature on official documents. The popular wisdom claims that this is how fingerprinting was discovered as a forensic tool: British colonizers learned that people in India used handprints this way and noticed how distinctive the skin ridges were in each print.

There's a reason the ancient art of palmistry is so, well, ancient!— and it no doubt lies in the fact that humans, from the earliest of times, have always recognized the unique, exclusive characteristics found in each and every hand on Earth. These characteristics may tell us more about our past, present, and future than we ever realized was possible.

A WORD IN THE HAND

It's fun to compare hand size and other features with friends, so many of us have pressed our palms together to see whose hand is bigger, who has more "graceful" fingers, or whose hands are most blistered after a long day of yard work. We tend to look at our own hands a lot too, monitoring how normal wear-and-tear cuts or scratches are healing, checking nail polish for chips, or washing our hands with particular care during the long cold and flu season.

That said, even the most fastidious civilian doesn't notice nearly as much as even a beginning palm reader. That goes for common sense features like skin texture as well as the more "occult" established hand shapes and what they indicate about our personalities and lives. Learning more about these features will help you look at you own hands and those of other people with more insight and clarity. Careful noticing is a huge part of why fortunetelling in general can help people feel comforted, validated, and heard.

A PICTOGRAPH TELLS 1,000 WORDS

Before humans began writing words, we started with numbers: More than 40,000 years ago, humans began marking notches in wood, bone, or stone, in order to keep track of time or quantities of livestock. By 3,200 B.C., people in the ancient Mesopotamian city of Uruk—considered by many archeologists to be the very first city in history—were using pictographs to record business transactions and keep track of inventory of goods.

These simple symbols were drawn on wet clay using reeds or sticks, and were the precursor to what would eventually become the first system of writing, called "*cuneiform*." Named after the Latin word for "wedge," cuneus, cuneiform consisted of many wedge-shaped symbols, which created a complex combination of signs to express an idea. This type of writing differed from pictographic writing in the same way a modern-day traffic-symbol sign differs from a written sign.

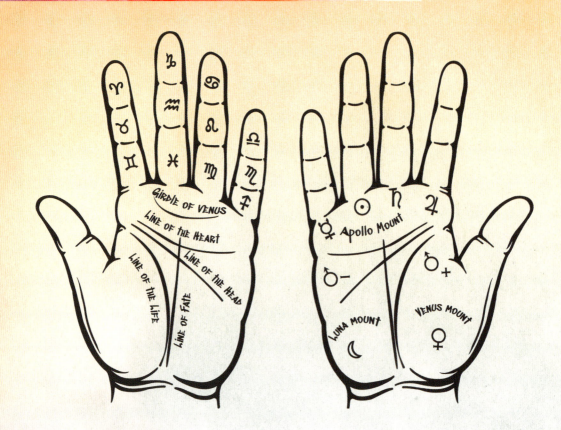

MAJOR AND MINOR HAND

Most people with two able hands have a major and minor hand. If you're right handed, your right hand is your major hand. Understanding which are your major and minor hands is useful because your dominant hand is typically slightly larger, stronger, and with fingers that are a little bit thicker than your other hand.

You probably use your dominant hand when you hold a pen, throw a ball, use a computer mouse, and almost countless other activities that are pretty mindless. Because of the difference in how each hand "wears" over time, the major hand is understood to change more during your life than the minor hand.

Palm readers may look at the minor hand to see more of what they believe you were born with, like mental acuity or personality traits. The major hand may show more about the kinds of jobs you've had, what your family is like, and more. For people who are naturally or forced ambidextrous—especially older Americans, who might have been "corrected" from left-handedness in school—or those who have injuries or handicaps to one or both hands, there's no need to force a determination for major and minor hand.

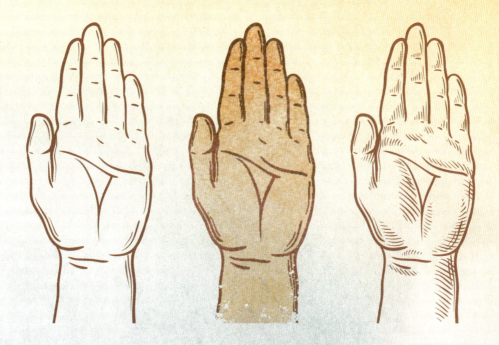

WHAT ARE WE MEASURING?

Without attaching any meanings, you can look at hands and see the qualities that palm readers use to categorize their shapes. Our palms can be more square, meaning fairly even on all sides, or they can be more rectangular, meaning longer than they are wide. Our fingers can be long or short in relation to the size of our palms. Most people don't have a textbook example of any of these qualities, but instead they fall somewhere in the middle of a spectrum or bell curve.

THE FOUR ELEMENTS

One famous way of separating hand shapes is known as the four elements system. If you're familiar with the Zodiac of western astrology, those signs also fall into the four classical elements: water, fire, earth, and air. If we believe palm reading originated with ancient Hindu people, the four elements were part of Hindu understanding, too, with a fifth element representing nothingness or void. Hippocrates called on the four elements when he made the first system for western medicine, which people used until the beginning of modern medical practice. The four elements fell into a hierarchy from most basic to most complex, and the implications for each hand shape are related to that hierarchy.

"Instantly I felt a shock running through all my frame; nothing was to be seen, and nothing was to be heard; but a supernatural hand seemed placed in mine. I lay there, frozen with the most awful fears, not daring to drag away my hand; yet ever thinking that if I could but stir it one single inch, the horrid spell would be broken."
—Herman Melville

Earth Hand

EARTH HAND

Have you seen the show *Avatar: The Last Airbender*? The characters inhabit a world similar to ours but split into large national groups according to one of the four classical elements, and some people in each group, the benders, have special abilities related to their element. Earth benders are the most grounded, using their bare feet to feel the earth's surface and its vibrations and movements. In the ancient Hindu tradition, earth is the basest element because you can sense it with all five senses. A hand with a square palm and short fingers is an earth hand. Square palms show that someone is practical and hands-on, not afraid to get their hands dirty (so to speak) in order to complete a task themselves. They like order, logic, and reason. Short fingers show that someone is effective and economical in their movements. They work quickly and often on many projects in the same period of time.

HAND SHAPE

When combined in the earth hand, we find people who work quickly and work hard, finding satisfaction in finishing tasks they can see. This doesn't suggest earth hands aren't subtle, skilled, and intelligent, just that they like to see, hold, and touch what they're doing and trying to accomplish. This preference can help them stay grounded and feel more secure, which in turn helps them be happier and more productive.

The Jewish folklore of the golem is a great example of a literal earth personality: a being made of dirt and mud and imbued with strong, protective magic to help it defend Jewish strongholds during times of persecution. Is there any harder work than this?

Palm reading, handwriting analysis, and onychomancy— "reading" fingernails—are just a few of a myriad of methods developed over the centuries as a means of deducing hidden information about humans, whether it be details from the past, a confirmation of the present, or a path for the future. And those who are said to be able to see, hear, or read such information are known by many names, as well: soothsayer, clairvoyant, seer, prophet, oracle, or, simply, fortune-teller.

Water Hand

WATER HAND

Since clear water has no smell, you can only sense it with four senses. In structure, the water hand is the opposite of the earth hand: long fingers and a rectangular palm. Long fingers show that someone is patient with detailed and tedious work, sometimes to the point of seeming fussy to those who don't have the same sensibility. Rectangular palms show that someone is motivated by feeling and emotion, rather than the hands-on practicality of the square palm. When combined in the water hand, we find people who may think hard rather than work hard in the traditional sense. They live primarily in their heads and love to imagine and invent. Many palm readers think of the water hand as the most introverted and sensitive type, perhaps artists and other creators who prefer their own company and to stay within their created and imagined worlds.

FireHand

FIRE HAND

The classical element of fire has no smell or taste. Think about it: fire burns wood and other materials, but what's left behind to create a smell or taste is no longer fire. Smoke isn't fire either. Fire itself is a chemical reaction lasting just the blink of an eye while it consumes one atom or iota at a time. The fire hand has a rectangular palm with short fingers. The earth hand and water hand are short-short and long-long in a sense, but fire and air are mixed, creating interesting new variations on earth and water.

The earth hand is practical and impatient, but the fire hand combines an emotional and imaginative rectangular palm with the confident, fast action of short fingers. We find fire hands to have sharp, confident instincts that they honor with their work and actions. Because their decisions are both quick and based on their intuition, fire hands can seem mercurial—another term with celestial and Zodiac origins. In the elemental sense, fire hands consume things quickly and need new sources of fuel constantly.

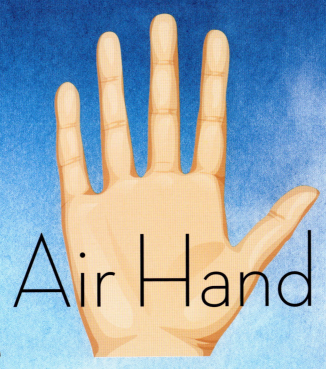

Air Hand

AIR HAND

Like earth and water are opposites, fire and air are opposites, and the air hand has a square palm with long fingers. Air can only be felt and heard, giving it loftiness and mystique compared with the lower elements. The air hand combines the hands-on energy of a square palm with the sensitivity, patience, and conscientiousness of long fingers. Where a fire hand can be quick-changing and temperamental, air hands are often steadfast in their ingenuity. As in the world of *Avatar: The Last Airbender*, air hands are the most rare and unusual of the four elements, and the most likely to be thought of as intellectuals.

In 2013, palmist Mark Seltman told *New York Magazine* that James Franco represents square palms with long fingers. Franco has made the news in a bad way lately, but he has always made wide-ranging projects that he brings all the way to market, showing an air hand's flavor of creativity and persistence.

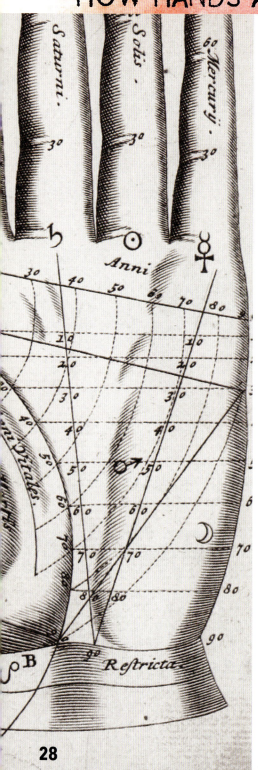

A HANDY FOREWORD

For all of human history, people in power have tried to suggest or even enforce that people with less power—economic, social, and even physical—deserved their powerlessness and were inherently flawed or immoral. That mindset trickled down into even the most intellectual crowds and the spiritualists and others who made up the palm reading craze of the mid 1800s in the United States.

For our purposes, we don't need to repeat flawed observations about how hands that reflect painful symptoms or other signs of illness or disability are associated with negative personality traits. That simply isn't the case and never has been. Our observations of how people present and use their hands necessarily includes this large, important caveat. If you have different or disabled hands or find yourself doing a palm reading for someone who does, consider skipping this section, and be mindful as you read the rest.

It's not hard to see that hands occupy a place of importance in traditional art, religion, and spirituality. But surprisingly, no one is quite certain where the word "hand" first originated. Possibly it came from the Gothic word frahinthan, which means "to seize," or the Swedish word hinna, "to reach." Since we can seize—and grab, and clasp, and take—and also reach out with our hands, it makes sense that these words might be the precursors to our present-day "hand."

BODY LANGUAGE

Our work culture places an almost religious importance on having a good handshake, meaning firm but not too firm, the right speed, and usually with eye contact.

Each of these factors indicates something about the person, we believe. Many of the same observations apply when you ask to see someone's hands at the beginning of a reading.

Are they shy, hesitating to offer their hands? Are their palms red or damp, indicating stress or nerves? Their hands may even be shaking.

Many of us have experience putting people at ease in situations like classrooms, public speaking, or jobs where we work with customers. Our instincts are usually good at telling us if someone is okay versus if they're uneasy, angry, frustrated, or impatient.

In addition, a person who feels insecure or worried about a reading is more likely to present their hands with fingers held tightly together, in contrast with a more confident or assured person who "hands them over" with fingers spread.

Think of this like the difference between a closed-mouth Mona Lisa smile and a broad, toothy smile. The thumb adds one more variable: if it's held nearly perpendicular to the palm, the person is likely independent and energized. A thumb held close or even tight to the hand can indicate insecurity or feelings of overreliance.

Somewhere in the middle is the sweet spot, where people are showing openness to attachment and vulnerability but still trying new experiences and learning with gusto.

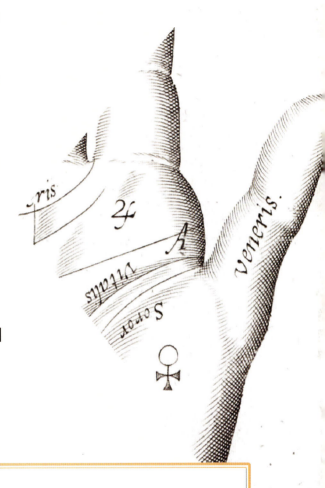

"And oh, my poor hands, how is it I can't see you?"
—Lewis Carroll

COARSE OR FINE SKIN

As with hand shapes, there are extremes that we can talk about as textbook examples, but most people's hands fall into a large middle area. Fine skin is soft and does little to pad the hand. Coarse skin feels physically thicker and can have larger, more visible pores or other marks.

There can also be red herrings, like someone whose hands are soft because they do hard work with chemicals that exfoliate their hands. Someone with a rising fever might seem flushed with health before the cold or flu enervates them. This is why any particular part of the hand or its condition can't stand alone for a reading, and it's why looking at the entire hand instead of just the palm can add a lot of value and nuance.

Exceptions aside, fine-textured skin is said to show refinement and sensitivity. People who work as manual laborers or other really hard jobs may have coarse palms and finger pads but the backs

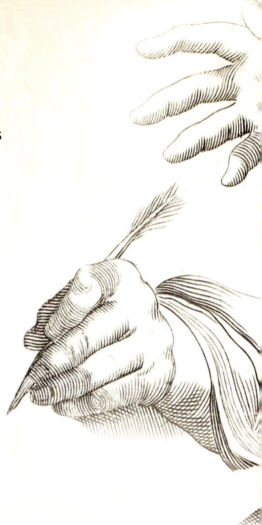

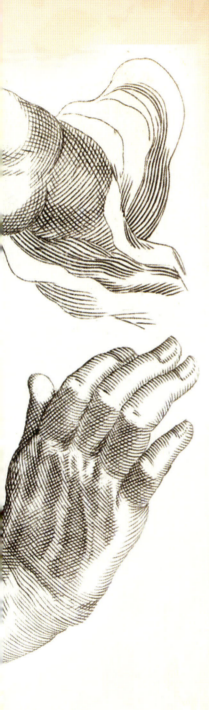

of their hands can be fine textured and soft. The work that people do can reflect qualities of their personalities, but this can be a question of which came first, the chicken or the egg. If you mention skin texture, be prepared to adapt your impression based on what the person tells you about their daily wear and tear.

Fine and coarse skin map a bit to the fire, air, earth, and water hands. Having fine skin may incline you toward sensitivity, but how that sensitivity manifests in your thoughts and actions varies with the countless other dimensions affecting the palm and the rest of the hand. Coarse skin can show that someone is tough, easily satisfied (in a good way), and resilient against criticism. Again, the best way to know if someone has coarse hands is to touch the backs of their hands, so you aren't misled by calluses or other occupational hazards.

Whether coarse or fine, our skin is very elastic and flexible, especially when we're young, accommodating our range of motion without bunching or growing brittle. Imagine if a synthetic product could do this without stretching out or breaking down over time. Our bodies are constantly refreshing their cells, powered by energy gleaned from the food we eat.

EVERYTHING
IS IN
YOUR OWN
HANDS

HOW PALMS FEEL

Have you ever gone outside after a rain and carefully avoided a big puddle, only to find the ground you chose to step on instead is sopping wet and spongy?

Sometimes the opposite happens, like taking a step on carpet that has no padding beneath. Either extreme can be jarring, and palm texture is the same way. When you hold someone's open hand and press on their palm, you'll probably feel an average consistency that's not too soft or too firm.

If someone does have very soft palm consistency, they can be dreamy and listless. But soft palms can also indicate someone who's very in tune with their senses and sensuality. They may be naturally gifted with skills involving hands-on touch, able to feel even tiny variations in, say, a massage-therapy client's injured neck.

People with very firm or hard palm consistency are thought to be more interested in hard work that produces results, rather than fine work that involves detecting very small details.

Some kinds of exercise will firm up the palms, so athletes may be more likely to have them. Those with firm palms can be more tenacious and constantly seek new challenges.

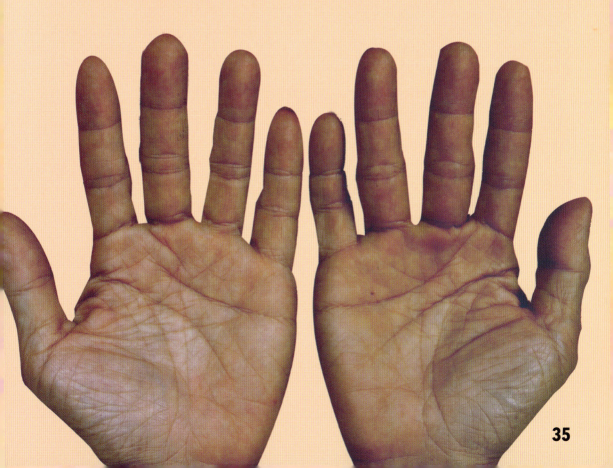

HAND FLEXIBILITY

Like palm texture, flexibility can change greatly over time. There's a chicken-or-egg question that it often pays to explore, because people with inflexible minds can grow more inflexible in form. Feeling rigid and frustrated can take a toll on our bodies.

Small-minded attitudes can reflect lives with a lot of familiar routine within the same confined area. And some people have inflexible hands or joints because of medical conditions—for them it makes sense to be wary and cautious and to maintain routines that work and help alleviate their symptoms.

When you're holding someone's open hand, you can gently bend their fingers backward to whatever angle is still completely comfortable. (We're forming an impression to think about, not trying to break any records—or fingers.) The most extreme flexibility is sometimes known as hypermobility, which can be a benign symptom that goes with a variety of other medical conditions.

Most people fall in the large middle area between very

inflexible and very flexible. Inflexible fingers can show that someone is entrenched in their thinking and can be very stubborn. Flexible fingers can indicate someone who is more able to think on their feet and adapt to what's happening. Have you heard miraculous stories of people who survived terrible car crashes because they were asleep at the time? Their relaxed, flexible sleeping bodies helped them avoid further injury.

But a balance between stubborn and flexible can serve us well. Some athletes have more flexible wrists, hands, and fingers as a natural product of their sports. Some work specifically to increase this flexibility. If we think of secular yoga as a form of stretching, it's clear that regular and sustained stretching can help some people feel more relaxed, in addition to helping build strength and flexibility. Finding stretches, pressure points, or other ways to exercise and relax your hands might help your whole outlook feel more relaxed and clear.

IN PHOENICIA

As early as 1550 B.C., the hand, or hamsa, symbol was appearing in Phoenicia to represent Tanit, the patron goddess of the city of Carthage. Over time, the hand became a symbol of protection to ward off "the evil eye"—a curse that was believed to cause injury or bad luck, present in many world cultures.

The symbol then became popular within the ancient Sephardic Jewish community, who called it the "Hand of Miriam" in honor of the sister of Moses, and the five fingers of the hand were said to represent the five books of the Torah.

IN ARABIA

The symbol also made its way into Arabic and Berber traditions, where it was called the "Hand of Fatima" after the daughter of the Prophet Muhammad. The five fingers once again took on significance, being linked to the five pillars of Islam.

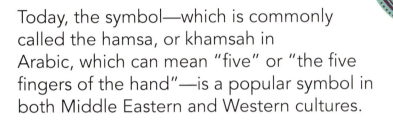

Today, the symbol—which is commonly called the hamsa, or khamsah in Arabic, which can mean "five" or "the five fingers of the hand"—is a popular symbol in both Middle Eastern and Western cultures.

IN INDIA

In India, hand gestures called "mudras" have traditionally been used in dance, yoga, and artistic imagery as a form of expression.

Each gesture denotes a mood or the character of a god or goddess, helping an observer understand meaning without the use of a single word. The abhaya mudra, for instance—an open palm, fingers together, facing forward—denotes calm and patience.

The tarjani mudra—a hand with the index finger pointed toward the sky—symbolizes anger. But when seen in images of the death goddess, Kali, her pointing finger is meant to aim harm away from the observer.

IN THE AMERICAS

The hand symbol also frequently shows up in Mexican folk art and religious iconography. Also popular in Mexican art is the image of a hand with a heart in the middle, which is said to represent charity, love, friendship, and truth, and to suggest that something is "from the heart."

Even closer to home, Native American tribes often used the hand symbol as part of their war paint, and the hand was believed to channel spiritual energy to the wearer. After a battle, a winning tribe would apply black handprints to their horses, signifying a victory. Riding back into camp, the hand prints would announce to all that the warriors had been triumphant.

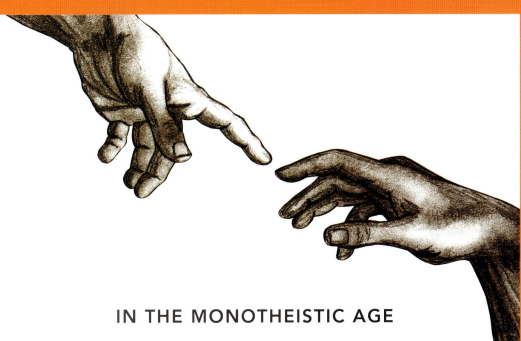

IN THE MONOTHEISTIC AGE

Although hands found a place of importance in pagan practices early in human history, the symbol of the hand became a sign of divinity during the rise of monotheistic religions. The Bible contains more than 1,400 references to the singular hand and more than 400 references to the plural hands, where their mention is often used to signify power and authority. The right hand, especially, is said to represent God's omnipotence, and the "hand of God" signifies God's guidance and protection.

Fingers are significant, as well: Christianity believes that five is the number which represents God's grace, just like the five fingers of the hand; and the ten fingers of both hands coincides with the ten commandments. Hands are also revered as tools to use for spiritual work, such as serving others, praying, or providing a "helping hand."

ARPENTIGNY'S FINGER TIPS

Casimir Stanislas Arpentigny (spellings of his name vary wildly and sometimes include the title of "Captain") was one of the most popular palmistry advocates and scholars of the 19th century, when palmistry took the western world by storm and had a huge resurgence.

He wrote multiple books on "chirognomie" (the French word for chiromancy) and other occult subjects. Where the four elemental hands were the result of thousands of years of classical tradition, Arpentigny articulated a new system.

ELEMENTARY

SPATULATE

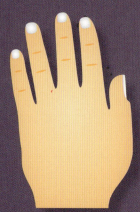

PRACTICAL

MORE DIMENSIONS

Instead of using only finger length and palm shape, he added observations on finger shape, hair on the hand, and how prominent the knuckles were to group hands as one of six types: elementary, practical, spatulate, conic, psychic, and philosophical. Because his hand types were described in detail, he added a seventh type called a mixed hand. Most people have the mixed type of hand, and Arpentigny's system was applied more like an enneagram, where someone matches several types with one overall interpretation.

THUMBS DOWN

Arpentigny's types give higher value to hands that fit stereotypes of attractiveness in the western world, especially devaluing hands he saw as "coarse" and basic, with shorter or stubbier fingers. In the context of his time, these observations fit into a sinister worldview that sought to divide people into nationalities, assign them immutable "racial" characteristics, and use those conclusions to discriminate against most ethnic groups.

CONIC

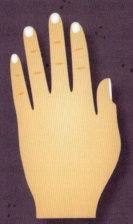

PHILOSOPHIC

PSYCHIC

SILVER LININGS

There are two interesting and inoffensive takeaways from Arpentigny's system. A hand with knuckles that stand out a bit is a philosophical hand, indicating someone who probably likes to mull things over a great deal before acting or making a decision. This doesn't make the philosophical hand impractical—this person still does accomplish things, they just take their time in a deliberate way. A hand with slender, delicate fingers is a psychic hand, which suggests the person likes to dream and be absorbed in fantasies.

BENDS, TWISTS, & SET

Some of the old tenets of palmistry have aged poorly because they're ableist or implicitly racist, but when it comes to the ins and outs of individual fingers, there are far fewer such pitfalls. If we consider having even, straight fingers to be the most average, this is also the least impactful arrangement. Having straight fingers is neither good or bad, and in palmistry, no news is definitely good news.

But what if your fingers aren't so uniform? Fingers bent or twisted by medical conditions aren't usually considered by palm readers, but it's okay to err on the side of caution without hurting someone's feelings. Each topographical feature like a bend or twist says something, and the message relates to each finger's celestial identity. We'll go into detail later in the book but a quick rundown will do for now.

JUPITER

The index finger is for Jupiter, the leader of the Roman gods and a natural name for the largest (by far!) planet in our system. The word index even comes from the Latin meaning pointer, like how the index at the back of a book helps you point to a specific subject or name. Jupiter's large size and power—both the planet and the Roman god—help to represent and signify our potential for growth and expansive kindness and acceptance. Good humor goes with Jupiter as well, including the word jovial.

The middle finger, or medius meaning center, is for Saturn, who fathered Jupiter and preceded him as king of the gods. Saturn is the god of forever, with the Greek equivalent Cronus as the root of chronology and other words relating to the passage of time. At the same time, pun intended, Saturn was intensely territorial and defended his god-throne with constant vigilance. His legendary dethroning by Jupiter ended a long period of plenty and contentment. The yearly festival of Saturn each December 25 was a natural fit to adapt as a Christian celebration.

SATURN

45

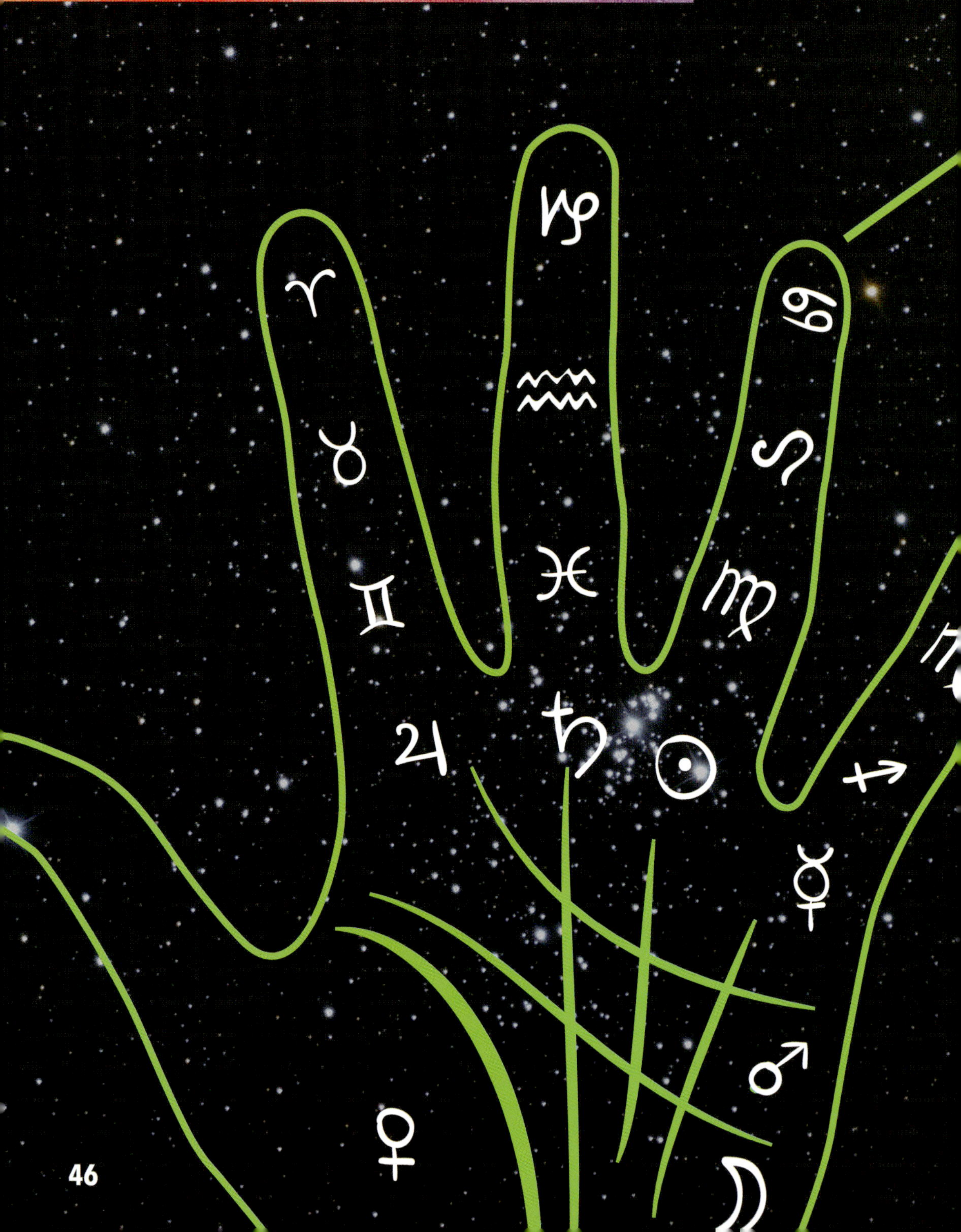

APOLLO

The third finger, or annularis meaning ring, is for Apollo. Although NASA chose Apollo as the name of its program to reach the moon, Apollo was the Roman god of the sun. Jupiter looms large over the other planets, but the sun is white hot and proudly dominant, creating the gravity and cosmic radiation that powers our whole planetary system. Apollo is magnanimous and generous at times, with the confidence and sense of intention and directness that only the sun could justify.

MERCURY

The pinky finger, known as auricularis in Latin, is the Mercury finger. Mercury is the messenger of the gods, so the pinky represents qualities like clarity of communication and social energy. The first manned NASA mission to space was part of the Mercury program, and decades later, NASA explored the planet Mercury for the first time with a dedicated satellite named Messenger. The name invokes first meetings, confronting the unknown, and forming good impressions. Mercury also speaks to our ability to coordinate different sources and paths to make things happen.

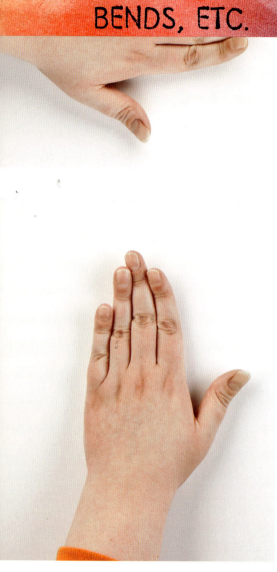

LEANING TOWARDS BETHLEHEM

Bends, leans, and twists come mostly in two forms: a finger or joint with just one of these qualities, in an extreme way; or a mix of two or more, to a less extreme degree.

When one finger leans toward another, think of it like a river tributary flowing into another river to make a larger, more powerful waterway going forward. There are only a handful of combinations of which fingers can lean toward which others.

Saturn is the tallest and strongest finger, and when Apollo or Jupiter lean toward it, they imbue it with their strengths and weaknesses both. A leaning Apollo or ring finger helps the serious, introspective Saturn finger to take a break and breathe once in a while.

A leaning Jupiter or index finger helps the serious Saturn finger to find confidence and energy to direct into its own success, channeling that powerful introspection into actions and follow through.

But Saturn can also lean. If Saturn leans toward Apollo, the creative and self-expressive Apollo can find it easier to make goals and concentrate on completing creative projects. And if Saturn leans toward Jupiter, the charismatic and powerful Jupiter can be more grounded and receptive to other ideas, able to use compassion when dealing with more shy or introverted types.

BENDS, ETC.

AROUND THE BEND

Remember when we mentioned the philosophical hand, where the knotty knuckles accumulate thoughts? A pronounced bend in a finger is similar, indicating that that finger's type is more pronounced and finely honed.

Where a leaning finger gave its energy to its neighbor, a bend is a symbolic collector of power that stays in the finger where it is found. If someone already has a strong Apollo nature and their Apollo finger has a bend, their creativity and free spirit may be next level, even to a point of making other parts of their life or personality suffer a bit.

Each finger's qualities can be taken to an extreme. If someone has multiple fingers with bends, this is seen overall as a rare blessing, even if the person's array of gifted qualities may add up to something that needs to be reined in over time.

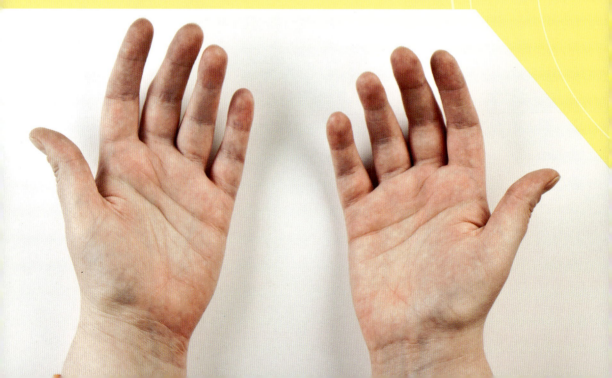

RUE THE TWIST

A classic twisted finger has a usually gentle rotation (remember, an injured finger doesn't count as an astrological quality) where the finger seems to face sideways toward the other fingers.

This kind of twist is seen as a manifestation of a lack in the qualities of that finger. Since each finger has pros and cons related to its nature, having a dampened quality can also be good or bad, making for artists who are less dreamy, practical people who are less rigorous or judgmental, and much more.

Remember how a leaning finger passes energy and motion into the finger it leans toward? This often leaves the leaning finger without much energy of its own, and twisted fingers and leaning fingers have this in common. The same finger is often both slightly twisted and slightly leaning, giving ite energy away.

A MATCHED SET?

As you learn about chiromancy, you'll probably stare at your hands and start to realize that shapes and attributes you assumed were normal are a bit more unusual. Children in school love to point out when they're double jointed or hyperflexible because it's a fun way to impress or gross out their classmates. They like to hold their hands up to see whose are bigger but that's just for fun.

The ways our hands really differ are more subtle and less entertaining at a glance. In an average or neutral hand, all the fingers are set at the same height, meaning they connect to the palm in a level way where no finger stands out. The arc of finger joints matches the natural shape of the palm without anything of note. Of course, plenty of fingers aren't set evenly or in such a uniform way.

A finger set high on the hand relative to the others means that finger's qualities are heightened, because the high set creates more room on the palm beneath that finger. The middle or Saturn finger, already the longest and standing tallest, can create even more aloofness if it is set higher. A finger set lower, like a twisted finger, means the qualities are diminished or changed.

Hold your hands flush together and you may discover relative differences in finger length, set, bends, and more.

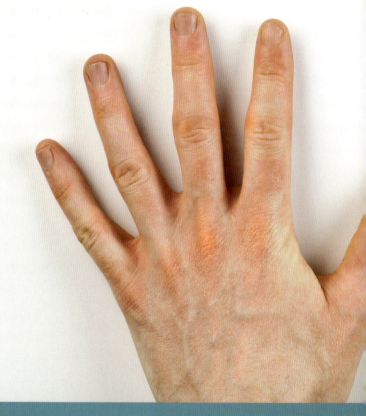

FINGER PADS & NAILS

Fingernails speak to our physical health as well as our lifestyles, personalities, and celestial identities. Today, fingernails are decorated with more technology and detail than ever before, including acrylic nails and no-chip manicures, both made from space-age polymers. But it's still super common to find natural or simply polished nails on people of all genders.

Regardless of race or ethnicity, people usually have nails and nail beds that are easy to examine, but keep someone's skin coloration in mind as you look at the undertones of their nail beds. We want to use chiromancy ideas to have fun

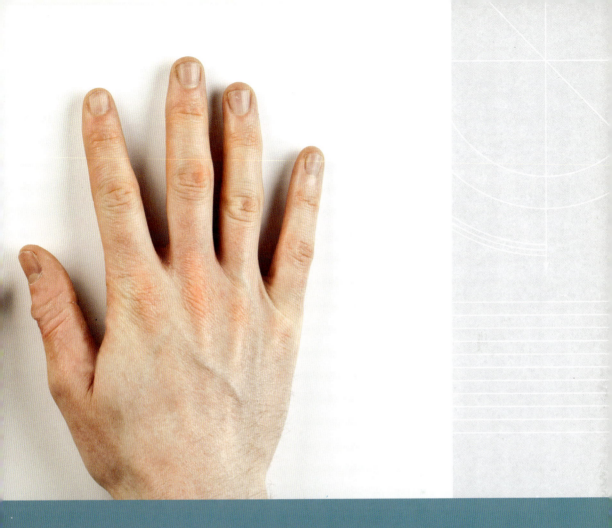

and spark introspection and conversation in all kinds of people, not prioritize one color over another or use ethnicity as a way to draw an insincere conclusion.

Most healthy nail beds are some shade of pink, and variations in color can be indicators of health conditions or illness. If someone has high blood pressure, poor circulation, or another condition that dramatically affects the look of their nails, there's no connection between that and their personality or horoscope. But for much of history, people in power have claimed to find a relationship between physical health and personality.

FLUID DYNAMICS

Nearly two-and-a-half millennia ago, the Greek philosopher Hippocrates developed a theory that formed the basis for how others practiced medicine for the next more than 2,000 years

Hippocrates claimed that our bodies contained four fluids, or humors, that needed to be balanced for us to feel healthy. At the time, there was almost no real science, and people made their best guesses to explain what caused health problems, weather, and more.

Our bodies are made of many kinds of cells that form solid tissue and many kinds of liquids, but scientists didn't discover cells until nearly 2,000 years after Hippocrates made humorism. Hippocrates also claimed that the four humors caused four different major personality types, each corresponding to a dominant humor in someone's body. In the meantime, wealthy people could choose foods that claimed to balance

their humors. Each humor was made by one organ, and each was assigned a profile like "cool and dry" or "warm and moist." Foods were given corresponding profiles and used to restore balance.

We still use words that originated as the four types: melancholic, phlegmatic, sanguine, and choleric. These four descriptors helped to forge the dangerous implied link between physical health and temperament or destiny, and humorism persisted into the 1800s.

It's not a coincidence that many texts link the four humors with ideas about phrenology, another dangerous pseudoscience assigning meaning to physical characteristics which ended up valuing able-bodied white people above others.

Without scientific knowhow, people fill the mysteries in their lives with their best guesses. Hundreds of years from now, future generations will look back on medical treatments like organ transplants and feel thankful for their improved technologies. But we can't feel too melancholic in the meantime.

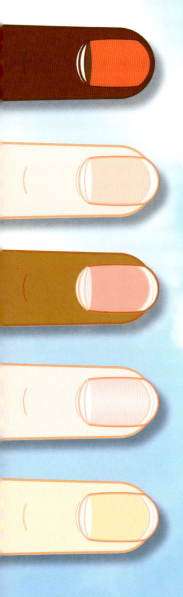

WHAT LIES BENEATH

If the average nail bed is rosy pink, small variations or shades of other colors are said to indicate differences in personality. A middle-of-the-road pink nail bed is good, in that it isn't a cause for concern or note.

This unexceptional color indicates good humor—a phrase that comes directly from Hippocrates's humor theory! With everything in spiritual balance, a pink nail bed shows a clear pathway from someone's astrological and chiromantic types to their expressed nature.

A nail bed which is darker pink and leaning toward red can indicate someone who is passionate and intense: the archetypal "hot blooded" temperament, but not necessarily with the negative connotations.

A pinkish-yellow nail bed can indicate someone who is moody, like a Saturnine personality. A paler pink nail bed can indicate someone who is nervous and somewhat cold.

PADDING THE DIGITS

Regardless of finger shape or angle, individual fingers can have pronounced pads. As with bends and twists, we don't consider pads created by injuries to have any of the same natural characteristics. Our fingertips are packed with nerve endings, which transmit fine detection of texture and other light touching along with sustained pressure and sensation from holding things or pressing against a surface. The loops and whorls that show in our fingerprints add another dimension to how we sense with our fingers.

Most fingertips are convex, meaning they're rounded outward without any dips or angles. A fraction of people have one or more fingertips with pads that stand out. Strong, pronounced fingertip pads on all the fingers can be a symptom of some rare genetic conditions, so doctors may check this in babies and children.

For people who are otherwise developmentally healthy, having one or more prominent fingertip pads is thought to be a sign of sensitivity, as though the extra surface area and cushion gives sensations a place to gather and stay. If all the fingertips have raised pads, the person is likely to be sensitive both in the physical and emotional sense. Individual raised finger pads can speak to corresponding individual senses.

NAIL SHAPE

For somewhere between 20 and 45 percent of the human population, one major factor affects their nail shape: biting their fingernails. Teens are most likely to bite their nails, but a large fraction of adults continue to. If you are or know a chronic nail biter, you've seen how nail beds can shrink over time. Not coincidentally, a short nail bed is linked with being critical of oneself and others, as exacerbated or reined in by other qualities. A keen-eyed critical observer can channel that talent into a career without letting it interfere with their self image or relationships.

A long nail bed, especially when it's narrow in relation to the fingertip, is similar to the water hand, indicating someone who may be delicate, intuitive, and sensitive. A short, narrow nail combines the critical and sensitive natures, setting the stage for a lot of suffering related to low self esteem or being overly self conscious. A wide nail that covers almost the whole fingertip can indicate energy, vitality, and motion.

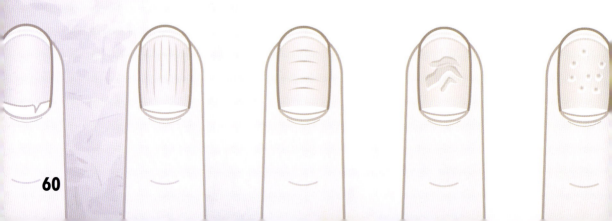

Somewhere in the middle ground between these qualities is the neutral nail, which doesn't have notable height or width but instead sits in proportion to the rest of the finger and hand.

The neutral nail is something of a cipher: on its own, it doesn't have a lot of outstanding or notable qualities. But it also doesn't interfere with how other qualities express themselves.

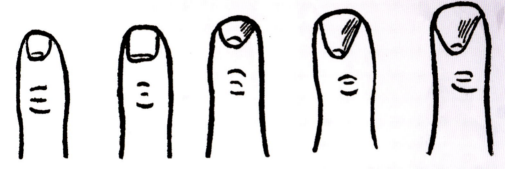

SHORT SQUARE NAILS. WEAK ACTION OF THE HEART.

SHELL-SHAPED NAILS. STRONG TENDENCY TOWARDS PARALYSIS.

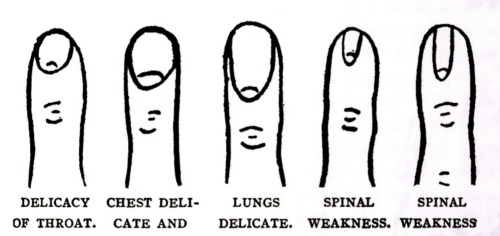

DELICACY OF THROAT.   CHEST DELICATE AND BRONCHIAL.   LUNGS DELICATE.   SPINAL WEAKNESS.   SPINAL WEAKNESS

NAIL SURFACE

For people who invest in acrylic nails or other salon services, their nail beds may be sanded down and roughened to help the fake nails or tips adhere better. These people must baby their delicate nail beds. On the far opposite end of the hand-use spectrum, people who play contact sports or have heavy manual labor jobs may regularly break or damage their nails. Nurses and others who have to wash their hands many times a day may have dry, brittle nails because of it. Even regular bowlers are likely to break a nail in a painful way at some point. Without these extreme cases, most of us can examine

our nail surface pretty easily. If anything, it's hiding beneath a coat or two of nail polish, which is easy to remove. A smooth, unmarked nail doesn't have ridges or white spots. From the side, the nail has a slightly concave shape without divots or bumps. The nail's tip doesn't bend toward or away from the finger; it continues at the same angle. This nondescript nail is the most neutral surface, indicating balance and support for the other characteristics of the hand. It's unobtrusive, and as the saying goes, no news is good news.

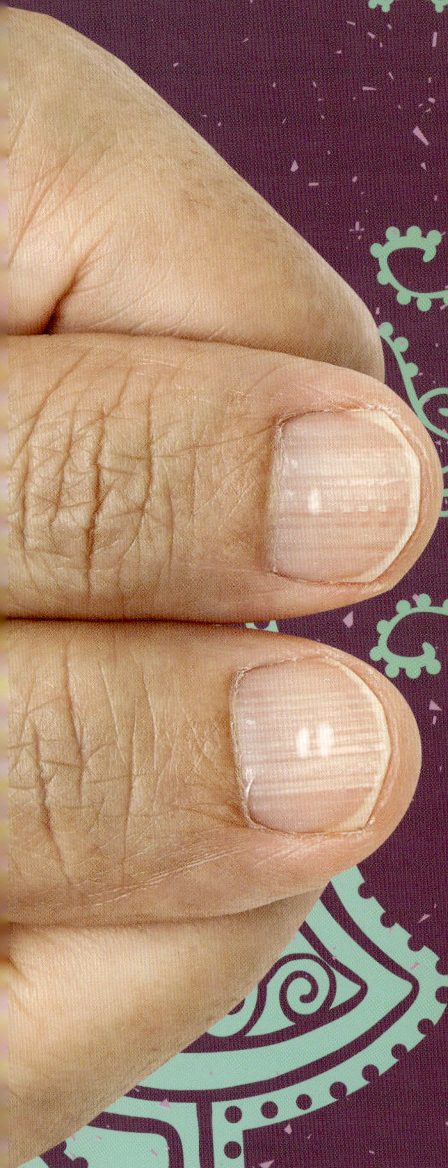

BUMPS IN THE ROAD

What if one or more nails has a pronounced ridge across it? Our nails bear witness to what has happened to us. If a ridge is especially deep, it can create a break or crack that goes through the nail bed.

IN PALMISTRY, THESE RIDGES CORRESPOND TO DAMAGING LIFE EVENTS, WHICH COULD BE PHYSICAL INJURIES, ILLNESSES, OR EMOTIONAL TRAUMAS.

Some events are big life stresses at the time but not all that major or traumatic in the big scheme of things. These can appear under the nail as white spots on the nail bed. If someone has white spots on many or all of their nails, this can indicate that they nervously fidget by drumming their nails. It can also indicate that someone is a habitual nail biter.

If someone's nails are fairly smooth and regular in appearance but thin, brittle, or vertically lined with tiny ridges, this can indicate that pervasive life worries are hogging the resources and nutrients that should be nourishing the nails. If this person tries to rebalance their stress level and find a more even keel, their nails may improve over time.

FINGERPRINTS

One of the most unique features of the hand are the fingerprints. Since no two people—not even identical twins—have the exact same combination of the loops, whorls, and arches that adorn the tip of each digit, fingerprints can be a useful tool of identity. We probably know of fingerprinting best as a way of catching criminals who leave prints behind at crime scenes. But the use of these small skin ridges as a means of identification began long before modern detective work. The oldest record of preserved prints dates back to 7000 B.C., when thumbprints were placed on bricks in the ancient city of Jericho, immortalized in clay.

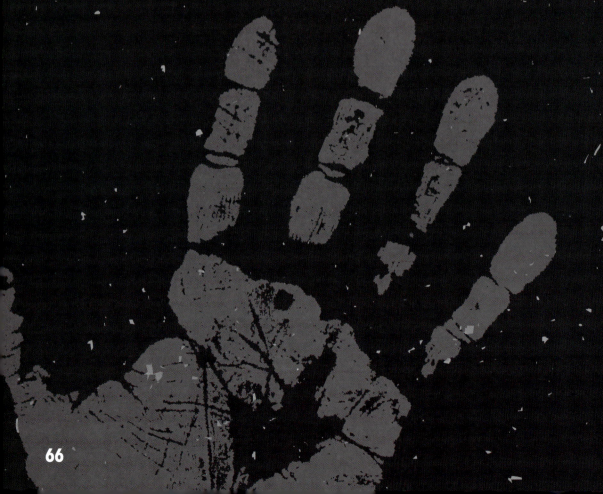

A MESS O' ANCIENT PRINTS

Although it is unclear whether these thumbprints were left intentionally, by 3000 B.C. Mesopotamians were deliberately using fingerprints on clay tablets to confirm business transactions. Fingerprints have been found pressed into the walls of Egyptian tombs, and prints were purposely left on bricks used to construct royal buildings. Many ancient artists—from Greece to China to Rome—left a fingerprint on cave drawings, pottery, and tiles as a way of "signing" the work they left behind.

SIGNATURE MOVE

In ancient China, inked fingerprints were used to "sign" important legal documents pertaining to loans, debts, and other contracts. The prints suggest that perhaps the Chinese were already aware of the unique nature of fingerprints. Although he may not have been the first to make the observation, by the 14th century, records show that a physician in Persia officially made note of the fact that no two fingerprints were alike. The rest was history.

CREATION OF THE WHORL

Usage of fingerprinting evolved further when Scottish doctor Henry Faulds and Charles Darwin's cousin, Sir Francis Galton, created a fingerprint classification system. Galton published the book *Fingerprints* in 1892, which described the very first system for classifying these unique markers, based on the patterns of arches, whorls, and loops found on each one.

The same year, an Argentinian police officer named Juan Vucetich set up the world's first fingerprint bureau, which was soon used to solve a murder—the first time fingerprints had been used in a criminal investigation. A few years later, the commissioner of the Metropolitan Police of London, Sir Edward Henry, built upon the classification system found in *Fingerprints*, categorizing prints with even more detail. The result, the Henry Classification System, became the most utilized method for fingerprint classification around the world.

MY PRINT IS MY BOND

Interestingly, the first modern-day use of fingerprints as a form of identification actually had its roots in superstition, not science. In 1858, Sir William James Herschel joined the East India Company and began working as a British civil servant in Jungipoor, India. To help reduce incidents of fraud, Herschel began asking residents to leave palm prints—and later just prints of the index and middle fingers—on documents. The locals believed that by touching the documents, they were more closely bound to them and couldn't break the contracts.

So Herschel used this superstition to his advantage and required anyone entering into a contract to leave a print behind. But in addition to preventing breach of contract, Herschel noticed something else: The fingerprints of each person were not only different, but they remained the same throughout their lives, providing a reliable source of identification. He even recorded his own fingerprints throughout his lifetime to prove this conclusion.

LITERARY MARKS

By 1906, police departments in cities around the globe were using fingerprints to solve crimes, including the New York City Police Department and Scotland Yard. But, perhaps ahead of his time, writer Mark Twain was convinced of the usefulness of fingerprints even before many law enforcement officials: His books *Life on the Mississippi* and *Pudd'nhead Wilson*, published in 1883 and 1893, respectively, told tales of crimes which were solved thanks to fingerprint evidence. And of course the most famous fictional detective of all—Sherlock Holmes—used a fingerprint to help solve a case in Sir Arthur Conan Doyle's 1903 short story, "The Adventure of the Norwood Builder."

LOOP

WHORL

ARCH

CONVERTING PRINTS TO DIGITAL

Fiction aside, the reality of cataloging and comparing fingerprints was slow, tedious work. But as the 20th century progressed, this became easier when computers made their way into mainstream society and prints could be cross-checked with databases in seconds. In today's age, nabbing criminals isn't the only way that all of our unique fingerprints can come in handy. Prints are often used for identification for driver's licenses, passports, employment, and for social services such as homeless shelters. Fingerprints are one of several forms of biometrics—including face recognition, DNA, and retinal scans—which provide a measure of security in many situations. Fingerprints can now be used to activate personal smartphones, laptops, and tablets, without the need for a password, locking out unauthorized users. Our hands can literally act as keys—and no two people possess the same one.

HEART LINE

There are four major lines that mark most people's palms. Two are roughly vertical and two are roughly horizontal. In rare cases, the palm can have just one major horizontal line, but for now we'll consider the vast majority with two lines. (See the section Single Palmar Crease for more information on that phenomenon.)

The topmost horizontal line is the heart line, and it runs just below the bumps that mark the base of each finger. In this book, we'll consider the beginning of the heart line to be at the pinky edge of the hand. Some palmistry texts consider that the end of the heart line, but for our purposes this is just a reference point to be cognizant of as you continue.

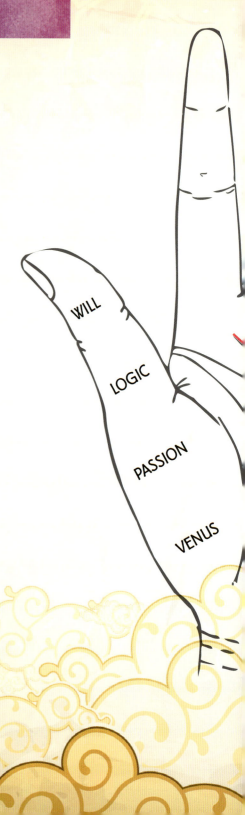

WILL

LOGIC

PASSION

VENUS

ACROSS YOUR HEART

The heart line usually wraps around the outside edge of the palm—the side furthest from the thumb. The other end of the line fizzles out beneath the middle or index finger, and it may end in a straight line, a curve, or a fork. Overall the heart line represents our relationships and our emotional lives, showing how we choose to love our partners, families, and friends and the quality of that love.

It matters whether the line ends beneath our Saturn or Jupiter (middle or index) finger or in between. It matters if the line is straight, gently curved, strongly curved, or forked. The texture and width of the line both speak to its meaning. And finally, the line may be unbroken and contiguous, or it may be marked by stops and starts that indicate our heartaches.

SUN

OF VENUS

MERCURY

EART LINE

NE

LINE

HEPATIC LINE

MOON

TS

HEART LINE

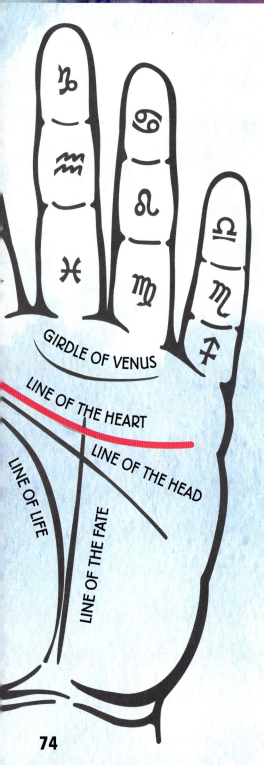

GIRDLE OF VENUS

LINE OF THE HEART

LINE OF THE HEAD

LINE OF LIFE

LINE OF THE FATE

WHERE THE HEART LINE ENDS

Remember that each finger has an astrological identity, so the position where the heart line ends is related to the finger or fingers it falls beneath. A heart line that ends under the Saturn finger shows that someone can be mysterious and opaque with their emotions.

They can be hard to read and may seem emotionally uninvolved. In romantic relationships, they may rely more on physical closeness and affection and leave their feelings unspoken, but a partner with a strong Jupiter-pointing heart line could draw them out of their shell.

If the heart line stretches to beneath the Jupiter finger, the person is likely to be far more expressive and outgoing with their feelings, which can also lead to overexposure and heartbreak.

The Jupiter heart line can show that someone is more of an optimist or even idealist in relationships, and definitely a talker who wants to understand what's happening in a friendship or partnership. They can find a saturnine heart line frustrating, at least at first.

If the line ends between the Jupiter and Saturn fingers, the person probably has some qualities of both the circumspect and expressive, making them more balanced in their approach to feelings and relationships.

These people may also be good active listeners, because they understand how it feels to need to be heard, but they also see the value in waiting patiently and hearing others out.

Balanced heart lines can be good foils for jovian or saturnine heart lines, or they can find comfortable ease with other balanced lines. As with finger length, hand flexibility, and everything else, a balanced feature is a good indicator that nothing too extraordinary is going on one way or the other.

What if the heart line doesn't end at all, and stretches completely across the palm? It's unusual to find this in someone who still has separate heart and head lines rather than a single palmar crease.

Without a clear finishing point, the heart line is a little bit unreadable. They may have

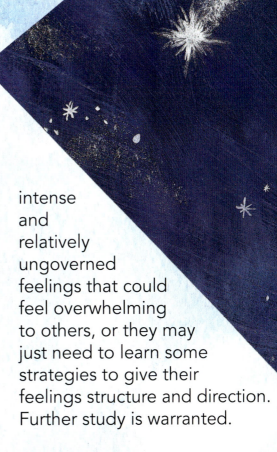

intense and relatively ungoverned feelings that could feel overwhelming to others, or they may just need to learn some strategies to give their feelings structure and direction. Further study is warranted.

WHAT A TURN SIGNALS

Heart lines can be quite straight, although a truly arrow-straight heart line is very rare. The other end of the spectrum is a heart line that curves upward, which can be paired with an exacerbating minor line called the Girdle (or Belt) of Venus. With a normal distribution, most heart lines will fall in the middle between straight and curved.

A very straight heart line is thought to indicate that someone is more thoughtful and cerebral in their emotional life—not suggesting coldness or calculation, just a desire to think things through and find similarly thoughtful companions. We can build connections with them by bonding with our thoughts and ideas.

A curved heart line can show that someone prefers to act in a physical way. With romantic partners, this could mean, well, what we think it means. But it can also mean the person likes to hold hands or lean against friends in casual contexts. Like an attachment parent or their child, the curved heart line can thrive on skin-to-skin contact.

A FORK IN THE ROAD

Sometimes, the heart line ends with a fork in two or three strands. A small fork that stays beneath just one finger brings to mind the same analogy we used to describe leaning fingers: like a tributary to a larger river, the fork intensifies the energy of the source finger. If the fork has two longer arms with different terminal points, the longer one will point to the more dominant part of their emotional energy.

In rare palms, the heart line ends with a three-pronged fork that touches all three primary ending areas: the saturnine, the jovian, and the neutral zone between them. People with this fork in their heart lines are compassionate to and fluent in the other emotional styles but are passionate about making compromises that serve everyone in a particular situation. The three-pronged fork can also bring good luck.

If a very straight heart line ends with a fork beneath the Saturn finger, the person may respond best to a potential friend or partner who likes to engage in conversation and examine thoughts and feelings but does not dwell in Saturn's potential introspective melancholies. A long, curved heart line that ends in a fork beneath the Jupiter finger may indicate someone who reaches out warmly with both hands, emotionally and physically.

BOLD AND BEAUTIFUL LINES

In the heart line, as in all the major lines of the palm, the strongest indicator is a clear, bold, unmistakable line that continues in one stroke.

Think of the line as a cable like the ones that power your internet or charge your phone. Do you feel safe and secure if your cable is missing some of its insulation and has bites taken out of it? If the heart line is bold, singular, and unbroken, this person has neither obstacles nor bottlenecks on the way to full emotional expression. They love and care without impediment.

Palmists believe heartbreak, lost friendships, and other life events cause visible weakening or breaks in the heart line, so it's unusual to find such a clear and strong heart line in an adult's dominant hand.

If the line is clear and unbroken but finely drawn and less

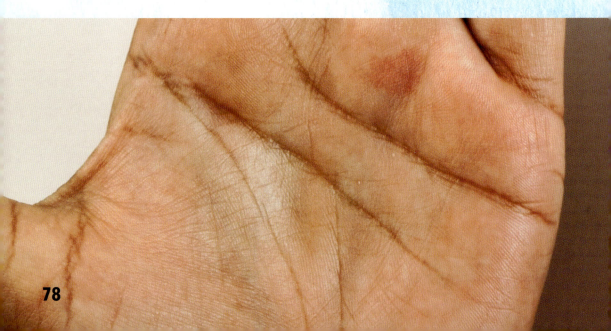

visible at first, the person can be hesitant and circumspect in their approach to love. Their pipeline does not appear to have much energy, but it hasn't been marked by life events. They may have acted out of fear and tried to protect themselves from loss at the expense of potential close friendships and loving relationships.

Rarely, there are two or more finely drawn clear lines that run parallel for the length of the heart line. People with this feature tend to be social butterflies. They can grasp tightly onto new friends or partners, spend all their time together for a week or a month, and then loosen their grasp and largely move on.

Their interest isn't insincere—it moves quickly, but it feels real. And they can sometimes have sustained connections, too. This just might require a concerted effort with a lot of structure.

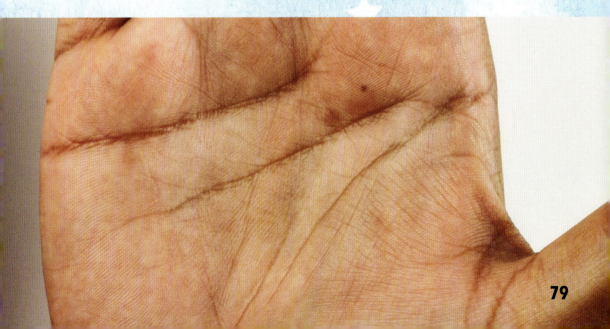

ISLAND CHAINS

If the heart line represents our life's worth of loving platonic and romantic relationships, any breaks in the strong single line speak to different experiences in our lives. The shapes or patterns of these breaks can mean different forms of relationships or kinds of aftermath, and the two most common markings are complete breaks in the line and small pointed ovals called islands.

Imagine the illustrations or photographs you've seen of the planet Jupiter and its large, persistent storm, the Great Red Spot. Jupiter spins very fast, which is one reason why its surface appears to have horizontal bands. In satellite photos, you can see how clouds flow up to and around the Great Red Spot. Clouds flow out again on the other side. In the meantime, swirling gases and particles spend unstudied amounts of time swirling in the centuries-long tumult of the Spot.

Islands on the heart line are like tiny Great Red Spots. They direct the emotional energy into a fierce and rotating obstacle, and eventually the energy flows out the other side and continues along the line. Like the philosopher's knotty knuckles or a strong bend in a finger, an island gathers extra resources to itself.

Knuckles and fingers link with their designated planets, but islands on the heart line are thought to be specific life events. Someone with a long history of troubled and tumultuous relationships with friends and partners alike will have a chain of multiple or many islands, and even, rarely, a fully chained heart line. If we think of each island as a bit of a traffic jam for emotional energy, people with chained heart lines must feel exhausted a lot of the time.

People in long, healthy monogamous partnerships may have relatively unmarked heart lines. But islands don't just mark times of romantic upheaval, and changes in family groups or friendships may also appear on the heart line. If any platonic relationship worries us enough that we dwell on it and feel stressed, there's a strong possibility it will appear on our heart line.

THE ISLAND

ISLAND CHAINS

THE BREAKS

If islands are the times we fixate and dwell on painful changes in our friendships and relationships, complete breaks in the heart line represent total losses. Yes, relationships and friendships end, and family relationships can be estranged, but breaks can also include when our loved ones die.

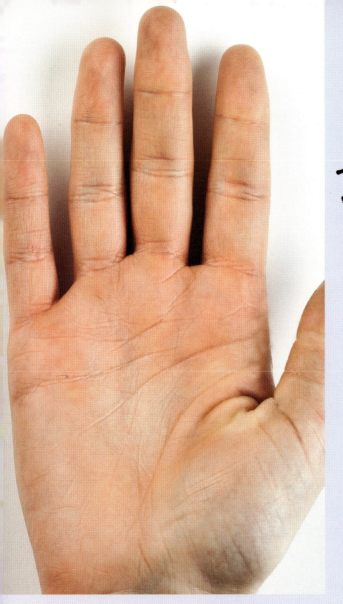

WAVY LINES

BROKEN LINES

As we examine the heart line for these breaks, and even for islands, it's so important to remember that everyone experiences even serious losses in different ways. There's no objective standard for what is able to affect someone profoundly, and listening with an open mind and heart is part of what makes palmistry a durable practice that brings people comfort.

If the happiest heart line is the strong, unblemished kind, someone whose heart line is broken in many places has probably experienced the most frequent and deep sadnesses. Most heart lines will have some islands and some breaks, creating a narrative like the tied strand of a quipu. Look closely, examine with care, and ask questions in a thoughtful way.

We have seen how hands have played an important part throughout history: From their first artistic representations in prehistoric caves, to their unmistakably unique fingerprints, hands truly are much more interesting than they would first seem. And our ancient ancestors must have believed this as well, leaving behind their unique palm prints and fingerprints long before language and handwriting gave us another way to identify ourselves.

USEFUL MANUAL

But those ancient peoples also noticed something else about hands: although all hands are unique and different, there are also similarities that can be found from person to person. During the Vedic period in India, which lasted from 1500 to 500 B.C., practitioners of Ayurvedic medicine began to notice patterns in the hands of their patients. Those with short fingers often seemed to have a fast metabolism; a long thumb was often associated with leadership qualities; broken lines on the hand indicated poor health.

CREDIBLE LINKS

And these ancient practitioners of hand analysis may have been on to something. Hands—and the lines on them—form very early during a baby's gestation, and some researchers believe that they are encoded with clues to an individual's future well-being. In fact, many recent studies have shown that our hands can tell us certain things about our health, our talents, and our temperaments, proving that humans have had good reason to pay so much attention to them throughout millennia.

HEALTH INDEX

Hundreds of studies, for example, have looked into the correlation between index-finger length and ring-finger length. In men, those who have a ring finger that is longer than the index finger tend to be more athletic, are considered more attractive, and have more children. Those with a longer index finger have the misfortune of being more prone to schizophrenia and heart disease; but they're also better at resisting temptation, and less likely to be autistic.

PRINTS AND IMPRINTS

Fingerprints can tell us more than just someone's identity, as well. Some studies have shown that abnormal fingerprint patterns—such as a higher-than-average number of ridges—can occur in those who will later suffer from schizophrenia or diabetes. One study even found that men with schizophrenia are more likely to have the arch pattern in their fingerprints, as opposed to the loop or whorl.

And criminals take note: the more salty the food you eat, the more salty your fingerprints will be. Since salt corrodes metal, this makes the prints of junk-food eaters easier to lift from metal surfaces. Whether or not this information will produce a rash of salad-eating convicts remains to be seen!

THE HEAD LINE

The head line runs roughly parallel to the heart line, wrapping around the thumb side of the palm and extending toward the pinky side. As the name suggests, the head line speaks to our intelligence, cunning, and mental stamina. In the late 1800s, the Spiritualist writer Rosa Baughan published a book called *The Influence of the Stars*. When the head line is long, Baughan wrote, "it denotes a sound judgment, good memory and masterly intellect."

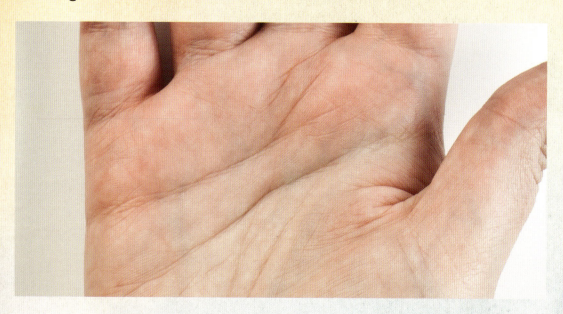

AN EYE-GRABBING HEAD LINE

The overall shape of the head line—whether it's straight or curved—speaks to the nature of the person's intelligence. A curved head line shows that someone is a creative and flexible thinker, able to change courses, richly imagine things, and easily make decisions on the fly. These are the people who impress you as much with their "soft skills" (making connections, active listening, being a good team member) as their pure knowledge. Their combined skills are valuable.

With our knowledge of the heart line and some of the hand's other features, we can start to build a bigger picture. Someone with a deep but marked heart line that ends in a trident has a practical and pragmatic emotional life developed during a life with a lot of relationship challenges and losses. A curved head line would complement their balanced emotional nature with adaptability and social intelligence gleaned from those same life events. What about someone with a very curved head line, a heart line ending beneath the Saturn finger, and soft water-element hands? This person may be so dreamy, introspective, and unfocused that they struggle to finish basic tasks without a lot of support and oversight. They may be very creative but lack the direction and energy to carry out their wonderful ideas. They may lapse into melancholy if left alone with their thoughts. Blessed with creativity but hindered by emotional heft, they may easily lie to cover their tracks.

HEAD LINE

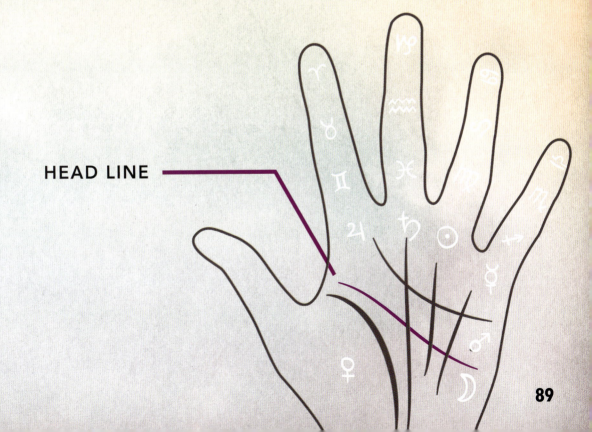

DIRE STRAIGHTS

On the other hand, a straight head line is thought to represent intelligence at an emotional distance. The person with a straight head line is grounded and rational in their

with a long, straight head line has talents and strengths, but they can also dig deeply into their own thinking and refuse to adapt, imagine a different or even better way to frame a

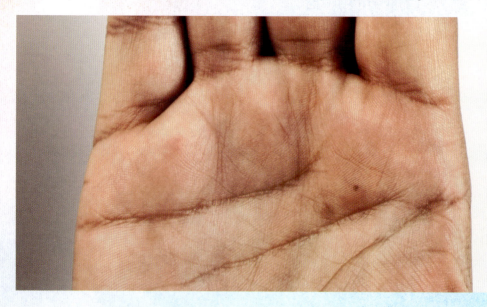

thoughts. They have keen minds for logistics, and an especially long and straight line ends beneath the Mercury finger, accentuating their flair for coordinating complex sets of demands. But a long head line signifies depth of mental energy and how readily we commit to our thoughts. Someone

problem, or fully consider other people's ideas. As with any strong, uncommon personality trait, people with long, straight head lines may spend their lives balancing their gifts with these susceptibilities. They can do incredible things, if they don't get destructively singleminded and absorbed.

WHERE THE HEAD LINE ENDS

On the pinky edge of the palm, we have three areas: the mount of Mercury, just below the pinky (Mercury finger); the mount of upper Mars, just below the mount of Mercury; and the rest of the edge, about half of the total space, is the mount of Luna. Whether someone's head line is short or long, it will point toward or end on the Luna mount, upper Mars, or a neutral place between them.

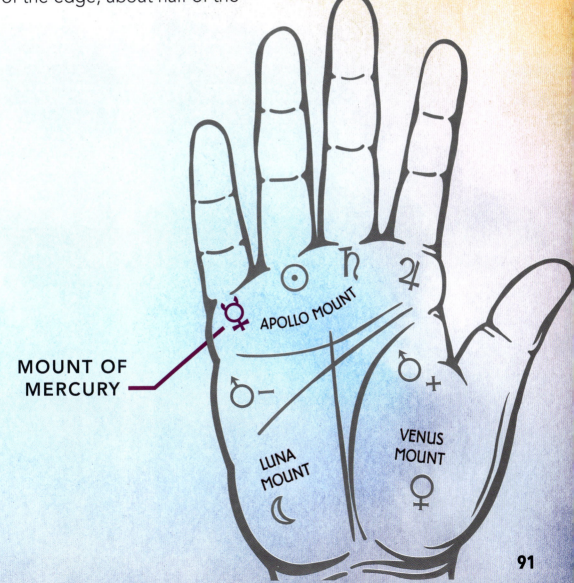

APOLLO MOUNT

MOUNT OF MERCURY

LUNA MOUNT

VENUS MOUNT

HEAD LINE LUNA

If the head line is short and points toward the mount of Luna, this person is probably easily tired by thinking, yet they're capable of great insights during those bursts of energy. When paired with the right tenacious and detail-oriented partner on a project, the potentially dreamy short Lunarian head line can help guide exciting work in an innovative direction.

A long head line ending on the mount of Luna shows the same ingenuity and gifted imagination but with a bit more staying power. This person might be committed to a career as a writer or artist or, depending on their level of interest in travel, a globetrotting journalist. With the strong intellectual nature of a long head line combined with the potential downsides of the Lunarian, the person may feel preoccupied with their creative work during their downtime.

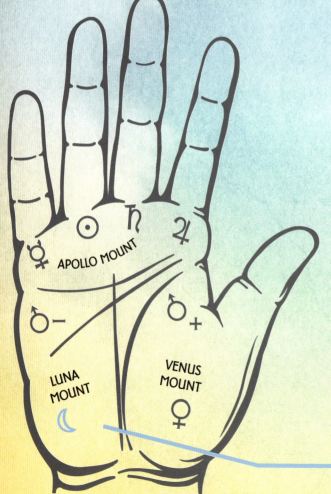

APOLLO MOUNT

LUNA MOUNT

VENUS MOUNT

LUNA MOUNT

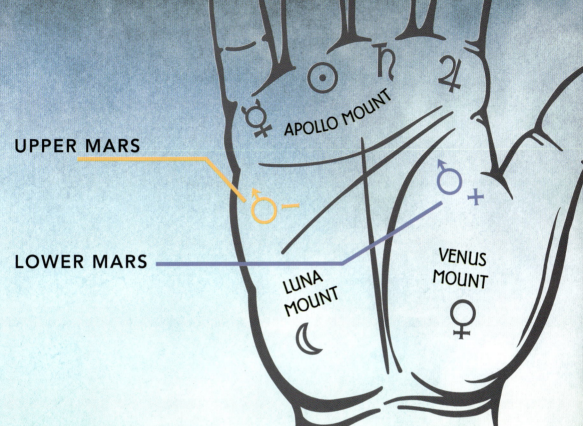

UPPER MARS

LOWER MARS

APOLLO MOUNT

LUNA MOUNT

VENUS MOUNT

HEAD LINE MARS

A short head line that points to upper Mars indicates someone who is probably brave or even blunt in their comments and observations but who isn't necessarily interested in sticking around to persuade others. They might be well matched for work as commentators or consultants, where they can connect with a company or firm that employs them but make sharp observations about other groups and organizations. With a long head line that ends in upper Mars, this person might be too direct or not temper it enough with practical or constructive criticism that people can use to take action. Someone with relentless blunt opinions that they feel strongly about could be a real liability. But the long upper Mars head line can highlight a person who is capable of crusading for a cause. They might find huge success as nonprofit fundraisers as long as the cause is close to their hearts.

BETWEEN MARS AND LUNA

A head line that points to or ends in the juncture of upper Mars and the mount of Luna is the most balanced and neutral position. Whether or not they have strong mental energy or imagination, these people are happy to walk the line between bluntness and nuance of speech, between long-term loyalty and something less predictable.

APOLLO MOUNT

UPPER MARS

LUNA MOUNT

VENUS MOUNT

A FORK, A BEND

No matter where the head line ends, it may fork into two or more branches at the very end. This can indicate that the person is more varied and diverse in their thinking style compared to the same shape and style of head line but with no fork. A dedicated, stubborn long head line ending in upper Mars will have a touch of the open-minded and imaginative. An almost flighty lunar head line will be more able to channel their bursts of energy into finished projects.

WHERE THE HEAD LINE BEGINS

The "average" head line begins around the index-finger-side edge of the palm, leaving no specific origin. If the head line does indeed wrap around that edge, it almost always does so between the mount of Jupiter above and the mount of lower Mars below. This is also where the life line begins in most people. We can use the relative position of the life line, which wraps around the base of the thumb, to place where the head line really starts. How far from the life line is it, and in which direction? It's common for the two lines to run together at first or for them to be separated by a very small distance. It's less common for the head and heart lines to run together for longer distances or for them to be very far apart.

ABOVE THE LIFE LINE

A head line that begins far above the life line may start from the mount of Jupiter. We remember from our discussion of the fingers that Jupiter is jovial, literally—the life of the party, with a strong feeling of caring for humanity as a whole. Jovians want to do good and be pleasant while doing it. For the head line to begin from Jupiter is a great auspice, indicating someone who is bright, persuasive, talented at making useful compromises, and likely to succeed in their life's work.

What if the line passes across the mount of Jupiter but starts from around the side of the hand? This person will still have jovian qualities like expansive thinking and a social attitude, but the head line's long distance from the life line can indicate someone who is very, very independent, sometimes to a fault. A small separation is the best, because having at least some independence is healthy and empowering.

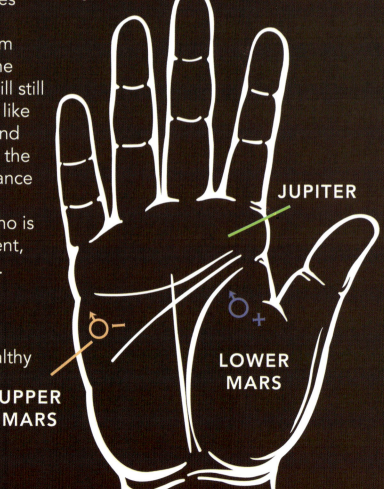

JUPITER

LOWER
MARS

UPPER
MARS

BELOW THE LIFE LINE

Where upper Mars points to the positive qualities like strength of character and loyalty, lower Mars, just above the thumb, can instead suggest more of the negative sides of the Mars type. Rarely, the head line can start from the mount of lower Mars and pass across the life line. This person might be hard to get along with, especially if the head line is long and ends on the mount of upper Mars as well.

A WELL TEXTURED HEAD LINE

As with the heart line, the "ideal" head line is clear, bold, unbroken, and relatively unmarked. An unblemished and uninterrupted head line shows that our thoughts are flowing freely with no impediments, and this applies to all the different styles of head lines. Even the shortest, straightest head line is able to think more clearly and concentrate longer if their line is bold and clear. A clear, unbroken, unmarked, but very fine head line is still good, but this person will have less bandwidth to take on heavy thinking or long periods of concentration. It's interesting to compare major and minor hands in someone with a fine, clear head line, since the line may be bolder in the minor hand. The events of our lives can reduce this bandwidth as our energy is absorbed in other things.

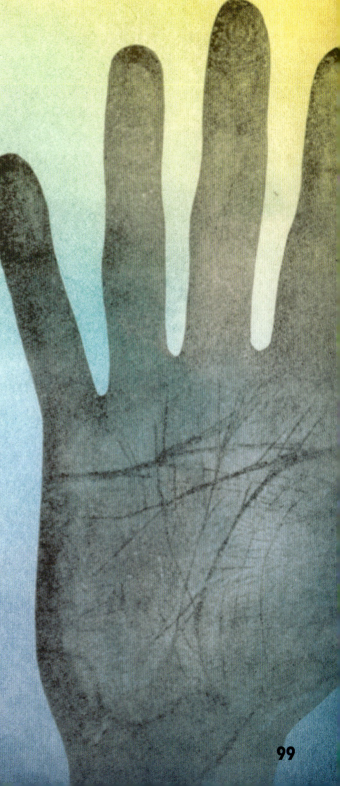

FLAT HEAD LINERS

What do we learn from a head line that is wide and shallow, made of multiple faint lines side by side or even a fine hatching? People with this kind of head line may be capable of deep, serious, sustained thought, but they don't enjoy it and they will resist it. They may have unreliable memories and be poor planners because of it.

Having a wide, shallow head line can also open someone up to be manipulated by others. Sometimes, this person can make sure their friends and loved ones are trustworthy enough that they can hand over this level of control. Others may find themselves stuck in situations where someone else has taken over their decisions or even their personal property or money.

ISLANDS IN THE STREAM OF CONSCIOUSNESS

Strong events or times of mental stress can mark our head lines with small, oval-shaped islands. As we explained with the heart line, these islands grab energy as it attempts to flow through, creating a bottleneck of slow movement that can impede our thinking and make it feel sluggish or even totally halted. Each additional island can add to this feeling, like tangles in headphones cables or skeins of yarn.

Islands can be narrow and tiny, larger and discrete, or lined up to form chains that can look like cross-hatching or braiding. Basically, the more islands there are on the head line, the harder it is to think something through in a timely way. If our head lines are marked by islands, we must be patient with ourselves. If we see these islands on the head lines of our partners or other loved ones, we must be patient with them too.

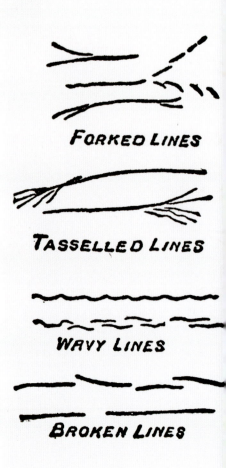

FORKED LINES

TASSELLED LINES

WAVY LINES

BROKEN LINES

SISTER LINES

ASCENDING AND DESCENDING LINES

CHAINED LINES

ISLANDS

BREAKING HEAD LINES

Where there are clear breaks in the head line, including places where the broken ends parallel briefly but don't touch, this person has a large mental obstacle. They may have already gone through this event or it may still be to come. It could be a mental heath crisis that impacts their life a great deal. It could be a flashpoint in a stressful work or creative project or the end of an intellectual relationship.

A break in the line is worse than an island, although a chain of islands can present as much of an overall challenge as a complete break. Someone with multiple breaks in their head line is spending so much energy just to think through their daily activities. Be kind and act with compassion. When we see a line like this in someone's palm, it might be rude to remind them of something they're already aware is creating struggles for them.

THE QUADRANGLE

THE GREAT TRIANGLE

The head line and heart line form a shape called the quadrangle, which just means any four-sided shape like a rectangle or square. With the heart line across the top and the head line across the bottom, the quadrangle's width is the area below the Saturn and Apollo (middle and ring) fingers. This area is usually slightly raised and firm in texture. Its shape speaks to us.

STRAIGHT AND NARROW

Width of the quadrangle is its most important feature. Whatever is going on with someone's heart and head line separately, at first we only look at how far apart the two lines are, not where on the hand the quadrangle falls. If the quadrangle's height is very narrow relative to its length, this indicates someone who isn't very emotionally expressive and may keep secrets.

The narrow quadrangle can also show that someone holds things in because they feel nervous and uncertain, compared with someone who keeps secrets to benefit themselves or protect others. With a saturnine heart line and martian head line, the narrow quadrangle may feel melancholy and unhappy as a general temperament, but there's no reason they have to stay in that emotional place.

On the other hand, with a narrow quadrangle formed by a jovian heart line and neutral head line, someone could be friendly and outgoing but with a tendency to keep secrets well. This person might be a natural empath and counselor whom others rely on to listen and keep their private information, well, private.

WIDE OPEN SPACES

When the quadrangle is wider, with more space between the heart line and the head line, this indicates someone who is more open in their relationships and with their secrets as well. As with any quality, this can be a "right amount" or it can be too much, since an overly trusting nature or sharing too much information can cause problems or obstruct relationships.

With a saturnine heart line and martian head line, a wide quadrangle might show that someone is too chatty about their inner thoughts, which may be pretty dark based on the mixture of planetary influences.

Some of the least likable people are those who hold court on their judgmental or negative opinions. They assume others not only want to hear these opinions but also agree with them on some level.

But a wide quadrangle with a jovian heart line and neutral or more expressive curved head line could be someone with an almost too generous nature who shares their creativity and thoughtfulness with true joie de vivre. They probably give their energy and time very freely and consider it a duty to help others.

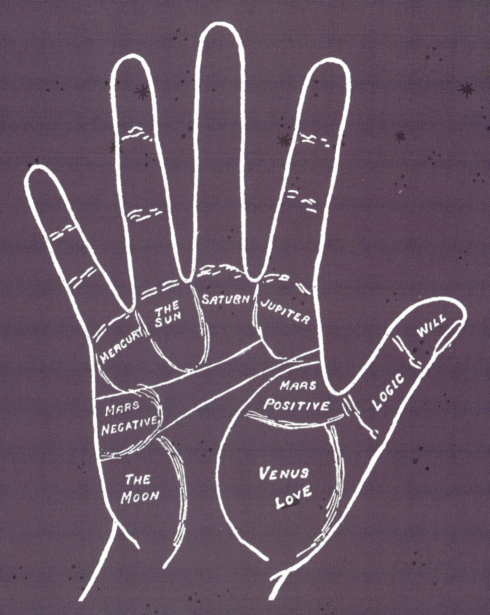

WHAT'S YOUR ANGLE?

No palm quadrangle is perfect, unlike the examples in geometry class. The shape will be narrower at the pinky side or the thumb side. Rarely, it may narrow in the middle but be fairly equal at the ends, forming an hourglass or bow tie shape. Each kind of shape tells us something, and most quadrangles will fall somewhere between these extremes.

TIED WITH A BOW

If a quadrangle narrows in the middle like a bow tie, this is often the result of a neutral or jovian heart line and a strongly curved lunar head line, qualities that point to a charismatic and thoughtful leader. The pinched area between the lines can suggest a tough time when this person's nature will cause or exacerbate a problem.

Depending on other factors, the narrow center of the bow tie can mean different things. The quadrangle may contain an angular bend because of a head line with a pronounced bend rather than a curve. (Think about an intersection of surface streets versus the long loops of an interstate exit.) Such a bend in the head line shows a big life change, shifting someone's nature from practical and sometimes narrow thinking to something dramatically more dreamy and imaginative. It makes sense that the pinched center of this quadrangle reflects a time of serious upheaval that has left this person feeling tired and uncertain.

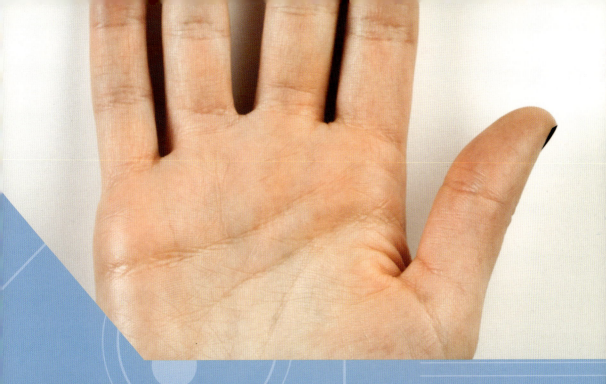

NARROWER AT THE PINKY

If the quadrangle is narrower on the pinky side than the thumb side, there's less influence from the upper Mars and more from the lower Mars. The pinky side is made of Mercury the messenger, upper Mars the crusader, and Luna the gifted.

A narrow quadrangle side is shortchanged on many of these talents. Instead, the wider end is lower Mars the aggressive, Saturn the withdrawn, and Venus, which can indicate an overly pliant or complacent nature.

NARROWER AT THE PALM

A quadrangle that is wider at the pinky side and narrows toward the thumb shows that someone is more in tune with the social energy around them. The moon, upper Mars, and Mercury work together to create good communication, sensitivity to social situations, and intuition about the feelings of others. With a narrower end pointing to Jupiter, lower Mars, and Venus, they may be less outgoing or expressive.

WRITTEN IN THE STARS

Using our hands to create words that convey messages is one of the things that makes us uniquely human. But some experts believe that handwritten words are also full of hidden meaning that express certain details about the writer.

Called "graphology," the analysis of handwriting is said to reveal personality traits and character, simply by looking at the way we write letters and words. And it may not be such a far reach to make this assumption. As children we are all taught the "correct" way to form letters—we use the same templates and textbooks, suggesting that we all should have similar handwriting.

Yet as we get older, each of us begins to develop our own style—flowery and flamboyant, or simple and unassuming; big letters that take up lots of room, or tiny script that fills a page; barely legible, or perfectly formed. Handwriting varies as much as the personalities of the individuals who create it.

IN HISTORY

Surprisingly, the link between handwriting and personality was noted as far back as 500 B.C., when Chinese philosopher Confucius wrote, "Beware of a man whose writing sways like a reed in the wind."

By the 17th century, the Italians became very interested in the subject, and Bolognese philosopher Camillo Baldi wrote what is considered the earliest essay on the subject, *Trattato Come Da Una Lettera Missiva Si Conoscano La Natura E Qualità Dello Scrittore*—or "how to recognize from a letter the nature and quality of a writer." Even today, graphology is still taught at the University of Bologna.

The practice then spread to other parts of Europe, where French priest and archeologist Jean-Hippolyte Michon was introduced to the idea of determining someone's character by their handwriting by a fellow member of the clergy. Michon first coined the term "graphology"—from the Greek graph, meaning to write, and logos, meaning doctrine or theory—in his journal *Le Journal de l'Autographe*, which he published in 1871.

By the early 20th century, interest in graphology had reached the United States, where it caught the interest of Kansan Milton Newman Bunker. Bunker was a teacher of shorthand, a condensed method of writing that relies on symbols and abbreviations of common words and phrases.

After taking a course in graphology himself, Bunker noticed that all of his shorthand students formed their pen strokes in different ways. He realized that it wasn't necessarily words or letters that gave meaning to the writer's personality, but rather the strokes of the letters. For example, according to what graphology taught, an "O" written in an incomplete circle with space at the top suggested a person who spoke openly and honestly.

Bunker checked his students' work and found this to be generally true, but he then deduced that the same should be said for other "rounded" letters, such as g, d, and q. Once again, Bunker looked through his students' writing and came to the same conclusion: The open stroke, no matter the letter, suggested an open, honest person.

Bunker went on to study half a million handwriting specimens and interviewed thousands of people, eventually creating a copyrighted, standardized system of graphology called "Graphoanalysis," also known as the American style of handwriting analysis. In 1929, Bunker founded the International Graphoanalysis Society, which today is headquartered in New Kensington, Pennsylvania.

Bunker's Graphoanalysis takes several different features of writing into account when analysis is made, including the slant of the writing, the size of letters, and the pressure of the writing implement. Some of the characteristics associated with different handwriting strokes seem to make perfect sense.

FOR INSTANCE, A CALM PERSON IS SAID TO DOT I'S AND CROSS T'S EVENLY AND USE SLOW, STEADY PRESSURE WHEN WRITING. ON THE OTHER HAND, AN AGGRESSIVE PERSON USES HEAVY PRESSURE, HAS ANGLED WRITING, AND CROSSES T'S ON A SLANT.

But other traits seem to have a more random connection with handwriting style, such as the tendency for curious people to highly place dots over I's and crosses on T's, or that those who are said to be kind tend to have handwriting that slants to the right.

The efficacy of graphology isn't a sure thing, and outside of television, it's used in the same ways that a lie detector test is used now. Regardless of its efficacy, graphology has been used over time as an assessment tool by psychologists, criminologists, employers, and even the CIA to attempt to ascertain character.

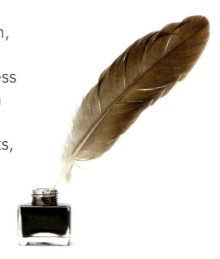

SINGLE PALMAR CREASE

One of the most interesting and rare general palm features is the single palmar crease. According to one 2015 paper, just 10% of the population have this feature in one hand, and just 5% have it in both hands. Men are more likely to have one or both single palmar creases. The reason this feature is studied by medical doctors and has its incidence recorded is that it can be medically meaningful.

WHAT'S IN A NAME?

In palms with this feature, instead of separate heart and head lines, there is one line that crosses the palm. Its unkind common name, "simian line," ostensibly refers to how some simians, which are the subset of primates that includes humans as well as monkeys and the non-human apes, have just this single line instead of the separate heart and head lines that humans typically have. Like our "canine" teeth, the term is scientific, not personal, but it does not seem neutral. We'll use "single palmar crease" instead.

A MEANINGFUL LINE

The single palmar crease is rare, but the people who have it are widely distributed and diverse. They range from neurotypical and genetically healthy to those with genetic disorders or developmental delays. But anywhere from half to two-thirds of people with specific kinds of genetic or developmental disorders also have a single palmar crease on one hand or both hands.

If ten percent of the population has at least one single palmar crease, but only about 1 in 700 babies is born with Down syndrome, for example, that means that of the 700, the other 60 or 65 or more babies born with a single palmar crease are genetically "normal" otherwise. The vast majority of people with a single palmar crease are not affected by a genetic disorder.

Furthermore, if half to two-thirds of people with genetic that means half to one-third don't. But the link between single palmar crease and developmental or genetic disorders is strong enough that doctors check the palms of newborns for their lines, along with checking the other markers of a healthy new baby.

Finding one or more palms with a single crease may be cause for genetic testing, especially if parents are already at high risk because of their age, family genetics, or other risk factors. Seemingly healthy parents with one or more single palmar crease may also seek genetic counseling to see if they're carriers for something like Down syndrome. This feature is just one of many tools doctors can use to help people gather information and make informed choices with their healthcare.

SINGLE PALMAR CREASE

SPIRITUAL UNIFIED THEORY

For palmists, if a healthy person has one or more single palmar creases, this line takes the place of both the heart and head lines. The existence of this phenomenon also shows how the lines in our palms, at least generally, are with us from birth.

We just discussed the quadrangle, which is the space

lines. If the single palmar crease replaces both these lines, we can think of it as the narrowest possible quadrangle. People with this line may be the most visceral of any of the quadrangle types, feeling their emotions intensely but often keeping them secret or at least very obscure to try to observe from outside.

THE LINE ON CREATIVITY

Reducing the distance between the heart and head can make single palmar creases some of the most sincere and creative people. Without any area of mediation between their feelings and thoughts, their expression can be more straightforward and with more fidelity. Their close link between heart and head may make it hard for them to moderate their reactions to the creative expressions of others, though, or to relate to how other people must work to bring their thoughts and feelings together almost as seamlessly.

CLOSING THE EMOTIONAL DISTANCE

The single palmar crease usually goes across the entire palm, wrapping around each side. If the line begins and ends in upper and lower Mars, this person can be not just stubborn but sometimes compulsively so. For them, this isn't even intuitive, because intuition suggests a link between heart and mind—not one single line that represents both qualities.

If someone has single palmar creases on both hands, they are the most inscrutable and complex. Remember that not expressing feelings well isn't the same as not feeling them, and not articulating feelings well isn't the same as not understanding them privately. These intense people may be served well by doing art or other creative work that values their profound mind-heart connection.

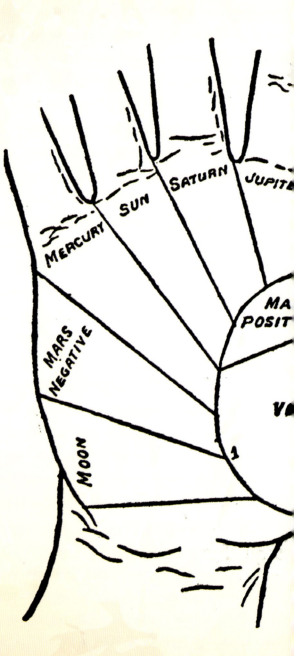

ON THE ONE HAND

What if the single palmar crease is on just one hand? We may also see one single palmar crease and more of a demi-single on the other hand, where one strong line has branches that point toward separate heart and head sections. If the major hand has a single palmar crease, this often overrides many other observations as to the planetary links or other features of the hand. Think of the delicate scent of someone's perfume or cologne compared to the strong smell of brewing coffee. One likely overtakes the other in a small space.

If just the minor hand has a single palmar crease, this feature is a bit more in the background. We consider the minor hand to represent what we were most purely born with, whereas the major hand bears more signs of the wear and tear of our choices, actions, and lifetime of experiences. Imagine the complex and wonderful inner life of someone with a minor single palmar crease and a major hand pointing to a fulfilling and energized life of creative intellectual work.

Because of its rarity and mystery relative to some other features of the palm, the single palmar crease can be considered a blessing and a gift.

OF VENUS

LINE OF HEART

LINE OF HEAD

LINE OF DESTINY

LINE OF LIFE

LINE OF MARS

LINE OF

OF

HEALTH

ACELETS

The life line may be the single most famous aspect of palmistry. "How long will I live?" people wonder, asking if their life lines are short or long and what it all means. But that's not how the life line works, and reading it is just as subtle and nuanced as the previous lines have been. This line begins between the Jupiter finger and thumb and makes a rounded curve toward the wrist.

It's not helpful to look at the life line as a measure of length of life. Even if we could reliably do that, what good could come of it? Giving someone news that is either bad (a short life) or overwhelming (an unexpectedly long life) will cause them one or another kind of stress. Most people fall in the middle of that range anyway, and remember that in palm reading we think of very average values as "no news is good news."

What, then, do we examine on the life line? It can tell us someone's level of energy and vitality over time and indicate periods in their lives when that energy is restricted by troubles like physical ailments or large life stresses. Think of it as the "liveliness line" if that helps. When someone wakes up each morning, how do they feel about their life? Are they lively with an upbeat and open attitude even when their daily life is hard?

WHERE LIFE BEGINS

On the thumb side of our palms, the Jupiter finger rises from the Jupiter mount, which is just the padded rise beneath the finger. Below the mount of Jupiter is the mount of lower Mars. Finally, at the base of the thumb, the mount of Venus forms the largest area of the palm. The life line encloses the mount of Venus and usually the mount of lower Mars. Sometimes it may also enclose part of the mount of Jupiter. The neutral starting point for this line, meaning the location that imposes the least influence on the rest of the nature of the line, is about equidistant between where the Jupiter finger starts and where the thumb starts. This is usually also the break between the mount of Jupiter and the mount of lower Mars so it's neutral in that sense as well.

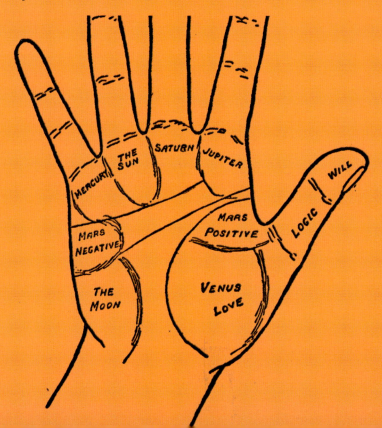

HIGHER JOVE

If the life line begins further up the side of the hand toward the Jupiter finger, this person's lively spirit will lean toward the largesse and expansive thinking of the jovian. Too far up the side and they can be bossy or even cutthroat in their level of ambition. People with this high line could have access to a lot of power in their work, personal lives, or even politics.

In her 1889 palmistry book *The Influence of the Stars*, mysticist writer Rosa Baughan explained, "When the Line of Life, instead of starting from the side of the hand, takes its rise in the Mount of Jupiter, which is sometimes, but rarely, the case, it indicates a life of successful ambition, honours, and celebrity— qualities given by the influence of Jupiter." Step aside!

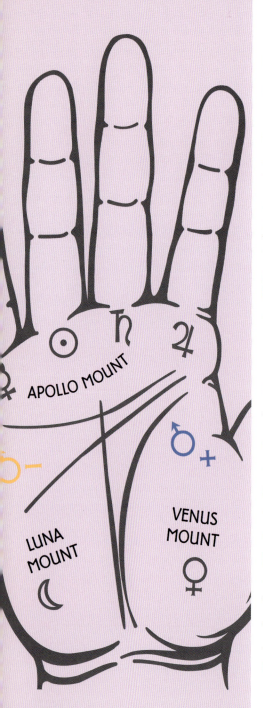

APOLLO MOUNT

LUNA MOUNT

VENUS MOUNT

LOWER MARS

If the life line begins further down the side of the hand toward the thumb, this person's lively spirit will be less ambitious and more straightforward. This isn't necessarily good or bad, indicating instead that someone may just not feel so driven toward specific goals or toward the accumulation of power. People with this quality can be hugely valuable and even vital depending on the context.

LOVE MY CURVY LINE

The average shape of the life line is already a rounded curve, like a clipped section of a circle. The powerful muscles that flex and constrict our thumbs are under the mount of Venus, and the average placement for the life line is roughly around this muscle mass. For people with this style of life line, their level of liveliness and energy is also average—it's not notably high or low. No news is good news.

In some palms, the life line covers much more area, drawing a circle around the mount of lower Mars, the mount of Venus, and some of the area known as the plain of Mars.

The plain of Mars is pretty neutral, indicating basically the negative space that isn't occupied by the mounts that ring the palm. But the larger area inside this life line indicates greater liveliness and vitality. Again, this isn't length of life but quality of life and quality of each new day.

If the life line instead cuts closer to the thumb with a shallower curve, the smaller area inside the line indicates someone who may feel lively and energized at the beginning of the day or when starting a new project or relationship. These people can tire very quickly, but they can arrange their lives in a way that helps cushion them from crashing energy levels.

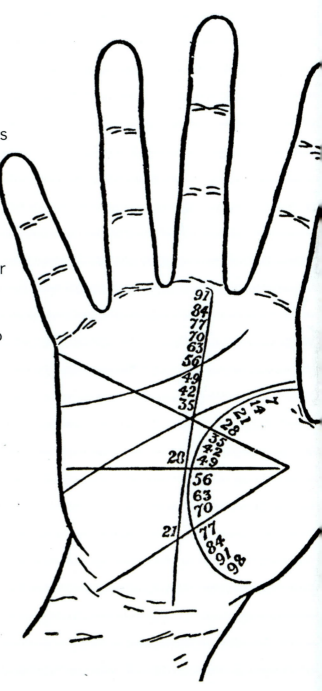

WHERE THE LIFE LINE ENDS

For rare individuals, the life line begins as a smooth curve but veers away to the mount of the moon. This exceptional feature is thought to indicate someone whose lifestyle will change dramatically at some point. Most other life lines continue in a smooth arc that ends near the wrist by either wrapping around the mount of Venus or ending with a straight line downward. The life line may touch the topmost bracelet (or rascette).

The closer the life line hews around the mount of Venus, the more of a homebody this person can be. This isn't related to energy, because a homebody can still have a vibrant and vivacious outer and inner life. A life line that falls straighter from the center of the hand down toward the wrist shows that someone likes to geographically expand their sphere of influence a bit more. They may like to travel for work or have multiple residences in faraway places.

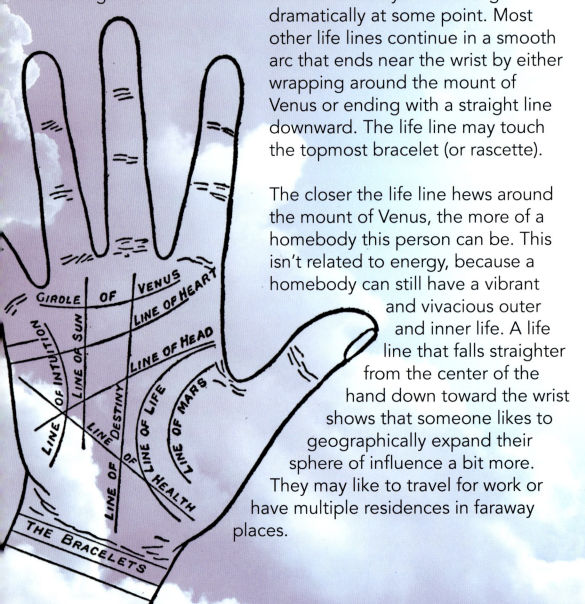

A WELL TEMPERED LIFE LINE

The most auspicious texture for the life line is to be clear, bold but not too thick, and relatively unmarked by islands or breaks. With a clear, smooth, unblemished line, this person is vital and lively with a deep pool of energy resources to tap into. If you know the business and entrepreneurship idea of giving oneself "a lot of runway" to become profitable or meet other goals, having a contiguous and clear life line can serve the same goal. No matter what comes up in this person's life, they have a smooth path to either side of any obstacle, giving them a constant and steady flow of energy.

FAINTER SIGNS OF LIFE

What if the life line is clear and unmarked but very fine or thin? Since the life line speaks directly to our real physical and mental energy level in a more concrete way than other lines, even a very fine life line that is still clear and intact shows a strong throughline for this energy. When we open up an internet cable, the inside is made of many small cables that all work in concert. These tiny little cables are still powerful as long as they're unbroken.

ISLANDS ON THE LIFE LINE

Unlike the heart and head lines, an island on the life line is the worst kind of mark, indicating a serious problem that interrupted and constricted the flow of life energy. Whatever the cause, the island forms a knot in the strand of the line, slowing energy as it wends its way through the extra length. The more islands, the more the overall amount of vitality and liveliness is spread thinner over the line's increased length.

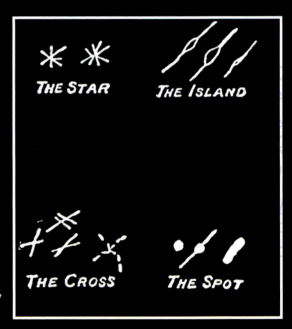

THE STAR

THE ISLAND

THE CROSS

THE SPOT

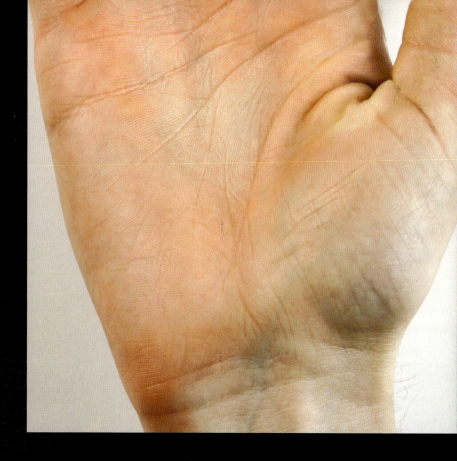

UNBROKEN

A total break in the life line does represent a big change of some kind, like a trauma that has caused a drastic pause and regrouping for this person. Breaks in the life line are often sheltered by nearby overlapping lines, creating more of a hatching effect than the Morse code appearance of a broken heart or head line. The line helps to shore itself up. During Rosa Baughan's time, palmists believed in the strict lifespan-measuring nature of the life line, assigning specific ills and injuries to features of the line and using its length nearly as an actuarial table. There are traces of this in some modern texts, too. But other palmists have adapted their takes on the life line and realized that its self-protecting nature points to our human ability to mend and move on.

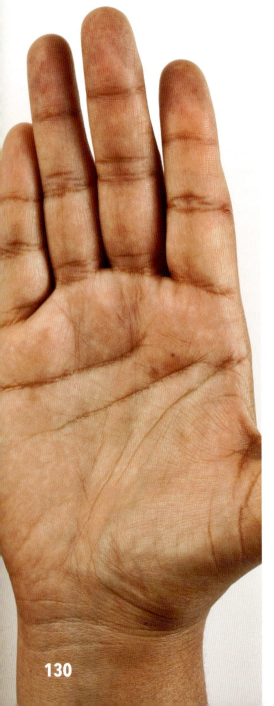

SISTER LINE

One thing Baughan and modern palmists agree on is the sister line, which is a faint second line that parallels the life line along some of its length, between the life line and the thumb. Since a sister line can be very short, there can also be multiple sister lines on one palm. When a life line is mirrored by a sister line, the person has a safety net for some of the time.

Especially if the sister line passes over a place where the life line is knotted or broken, it acts like an energy bypass, allowing liveliness and vitality to pass through the sister line without getting stuck in the twists and obstacles on the life line itself. Like a real sister, the helper line can make life easier by lightening the load.

For the heart and head lines, a little river of faint lines side by side is pretty innocuous, indicating that someone might be flaky or flighty in those qualities but not harmful. If the life line is this kind of shallow ribbon, it can be more serious.

The ideal life line is clear and bold, making a handful of faint, barely distinguishable lines the direct opposite. With no firm channel to travel through, this person's vitality and liveliness can drain out. The life line may also grow faint in parts but not for its whole length. Instead of the dramatic impact of an island or a break in the line, these faint spots point to times of low energy, not totally depleted or nonexistent energy.

It's normal to see a variety of features on the life line, indicating a full life of varied experiences that have drained and restarted someone's battery over the many years of life.

A HAND BY ANY OTHER NAME

The name for the palm of the hand comes from the Latin palma, which is also the source for the name of the palm tree. In fact, the name for the tree was secondary—and it can thank the shape of a hand for its moniker: the clusters of leaves on a palm branch fan out, reminiscent of the fingers on a hand. English is full of sayings and idioms that include "hand" or "palm," underscoring the significance these small— but incredibly useful— appendages. Don't bite the hand that feeds you; living hand to mouth; have the upper hand; a heavy hand; itchy palm; you've got him in the palm of your hand; and literally dozens more.

King Lear was immortalized most famously by William Shakespeare, but Leir, the original legend from British mythology, was brought out of the ether in the 12th century by the Welsh-born fabulist Geoffrey of Monmouth.

"O irreversible decrees of the Fates, that never swerve from your stated course!" Geoffrey's Leir laments. "Why did you ever advance me to an unstable felicity, since the punishment of lost happiness is greater than the sense of present misery?"

In a way, legends like King Leir and Oedipus Rex highlight the dangers of fate. How do we choose for ourselves when we're pressed in place by the unseen but heavily felt weight of destiny? Oedipus tries to fight against his prophecy but just confirms it in the end.

On the other hand, Leir has done what's expected of him as an aging king, but his terrible outcomes lead him to begin making a new plan. After his complaining above, Leir takes refuge with his one loyal daughter and they wrest his kingdom back from corrupt usurpers. He takes his fate back.

ON THE HAND, IN THE STARS

The destiny line, which traces vertically down the center of the palm, is the first line we'll discuss that is completely optional. If we indeed count a single palmar crease as both the heart and head line for its bearers, everyone has these two lines and a life line.

Not everyone has a destiny line, and each one can vary significantly more than the first three major lines. To see a "textbook" destiny line that extends straight from the top of the palm to the bottom is really unusual. In fact, it's more common to find no destiny line than one this long.

Most destiny lines are short, striking through one or two of the major lines before fading. Where the destiny line starts and ends is important, as is where and how it overlaps the other lines of the palm. If the destiny line in the major hand is hard to trace, compare with the minor hand to see if that brings more details to light.

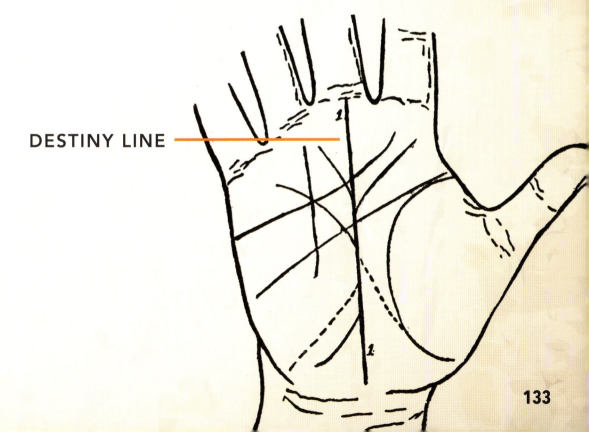

DESTINY LINE

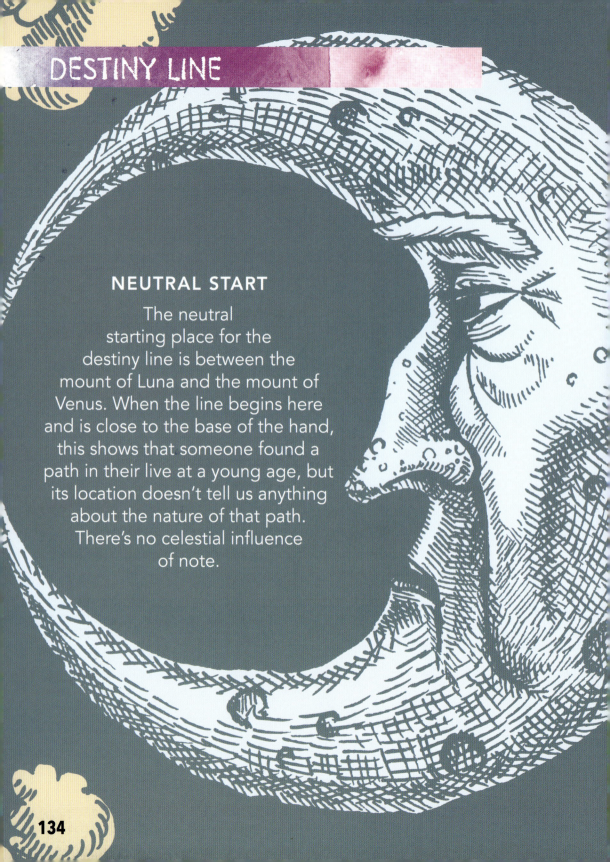

NEUTRAL START

The neutral starting place for the destiny line is between the mount of Luna and the mount of Venus. When the line begins here and is close to the base of the hand, this shows that someone found a path in their live at a young age, but its location doesn't tell us anything about the nature of that path. There's no celestial influence of note.

OVERLAPPING LIFE

If the destiny line begins with the life line and eventually branches away, this person has probably been led toward a path by someone in their family. This could be a family business the person is excited to take over someday, a feeling of admiration for parents or grandparents who worked in public service or politics, or even a childhood filled with stressful pressure to become a doctor. The line is value neutral.

The line can also begin on the mount of Venus and cross the life line. This person may have even stronger influences, like circumstances that require them to rely on their family financially more than they'd prefer. Someone with a family-linked destiny line early in life can turn this sign into just about anything as they grow older, but this context can be important no matter their adult path.

LUNAR DESTINY

Beginning on the mount of Luna, the destiny line speaks less to family involvement and more to a generally nurturing environment all around. This person can be very creative and feel drawn to the arts or other expressive careers, including using their talents for the greater good. The destiny line from the mount of Luna may find rewarding work as a grant writer or public artist.

ENDING IN SATURN

Some palmists call the destiny line the "line of Saturn." In fact, no matter where they begin, all destiny lines point toward or end on the mount of Saturn beneath the Saturn (or middle) finger. Remember that Saturn can be melancholy and self critical, but it is also capable of great self reflection, expansive thoughts about the nature of life and the universe, and careful decision making with career choices, money, and more. In the section "Of the Saturnia, or Line of Saturn," the anonymous author of 1885's *The Witches's Dream Book and Fortune Teller* writes, "This being wholly and fully protracted to the middle finger, is an argument both of profound cogitations and likewise of fortunate events in counsels in actions." In other words, a high-quality destiny line indicates someone who thinks clearly and deeply, makes good decisions, and chooses good people to ask for help or advice. If that weren't enough, they're also lucky.

LENGTH OF DESTINY LINE

We've said that a long, "ideal" destiny line is unusual— even discussing it is more of a comparison point for the real destiny lines we'll see on people's palms. But what do the lengths of destiny lines mean? What if they stop and start in skips and jumps? With this unpredictable line, we need to be prepared for anything.

The closer the destiny line is to the base of the hand, the earlier in their life the line is describing. The line could begin here, fade away for a time, then reappear further up the palm. With the heart or head line, such a gap is a cause for serious reflection and care, indicating some kind of accident or other life trauma that interrupted someone's development or inner life. The destiny line does no such doomsaying.

UNCLEAR DESTINY

When the destiny line is missing a section, this can speak to a time when someone was less secure or safe in their life, and in that sense it can be a serious indicator. But most of the time, these gaps are times when people felt a little lost, considered a change in career or life calling, or disconnected from their professional life to make personal changes like starting a family. This is why a clear, long, unmarked destiny line is so truly rare: almost no one lives such a rigid and structured life, and that's a good thing. People who totally lack destiny lines can still find great financial and professional success, like the venture capitalists who move on to new projects every few months and never know for sure how an investment will turn out.

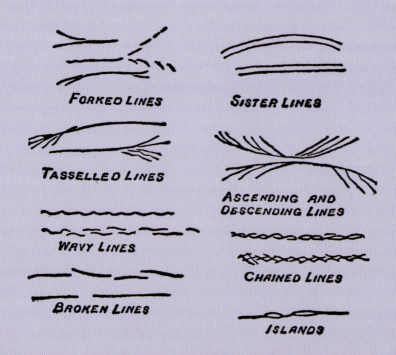

FORKED LINES

SISTER LINES

TASSELLED LINES

ASCENDING AND DESCENDING LINES

WAVY LINES

CHAINED LINES

BROKEN LINES

ISLANDS

CHANGED DESTINY

We discussed how the destiny line can begin very low on the palm, almost at the wrist, indicating that someone's childhood was hemmed in by family expectations in one way or another. It's common to see this early destiny line with a large gap further up the hand when the person had to grapple with a real life that didn't match what they were led to believe. This can be difficult, but for some it is also a relief to feel independent.

DESTINY WELL MARKED

The destiny line may skip and dash up our palms, but it should still be easily visible and clear on the palm when it does appear. With a bold segment in someone's destiny line, we know their path during this time will help them feel safe and secure, no matter what the path itself means for their work or life choices. And conversely, if a segment is missing, it's best that it is completely missing rather than faintly lined and just visible.

THE RISE OF PALMISTRY

Today scientists agree that our hands can provide us with some invaluable information. But when palmistry—which had been a respected practice since antiquity in India, China, and the Middle East—made its way to Europe in the Middle Ages, the method was considered superstition and a form of witchcraft condemned by the Catholic Church.

During the Renaissance, palmistry was called a "forbidden art," and for centuries those who practiced it did so in secret. The famed King Henry VIII once called it "a crafty means to deceive people," but his attitude was not shared by the common people of the time. Regular folks still loved and believed in palmistry.

So, despite the official condemnation of the practice, palmistry began to flourish in underground channels; many texts and illustrations were published during the 16th and 17th centuries describing the methods for studying hands and showing diagrams which detailed each area of significance.

Books such as George Wharton's *The Art of Divining by the Lines and Signature Ingraven on the Hand of Man*, which was published in 1652, increased interest in the methods used for reading palms.

But it was the Roma people, also called Travelers or the deprecated term "gypsies," who truly brought the practice back to popularity in Europe. In fact, the Roma are so closely associated with palm reading that many of us automatically think of the Roma when we hear the term. The Roma people originated in India around 1500 years ago, then migrated north to the Balkan Mountains and from there began travelling through Europe. Their nomadic lifestyle, unique dress and language, and propensity to keep to themselves has often made them a target of distrust and bigotry. Always on the move, The Roma earned money by finding odd jobs, playing games of chance, and, of course, fortune-telling. And even those who looked to the Roma with a wary eye would often visit them during times of trouble, due to their reputation for divining the secrets we hold in our hands.

Palm reading has always been popular amongst the Roma, so much so that some say Roma mothers taught their children how to palm read at a very early age. Since it doesn't require any special equipment and can be practiced any time and any place, the skill was easily passed down from parents to children, enabling entire families to have means of income.

In 1820, a young Roma girl happened to read the palm of Captain Casimir Stanislas D'Arpentigny, a French army officer who was serving in Spain during the Peninsular War. This single chance encounter led to a revival of palmistry throughout Europe, and helped to bring it out of the shadows and into the mainstream.

D'Arpentigny was so fascinated by his palm reading that he began paying close attention to the hands of his friends and acquaintances. One of his first observations concerned the finger joints of guests at a party: He noted that those who were scientists, engineers, and mathematicians tended to have knotty joints, whereas the joints of artists, poets, and musicians were relatively smooth.

He concluded that these differences must correspond

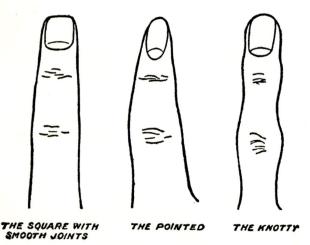

THE SQUARE WITH SMOOTH JOINTS   THE POINTED   THE KNOTTY

to each person's personality. D'Arpentigny also began cataloging different hand shapes, developing a classification system for them. In 1839 he published all his research and observations in the book, *La*

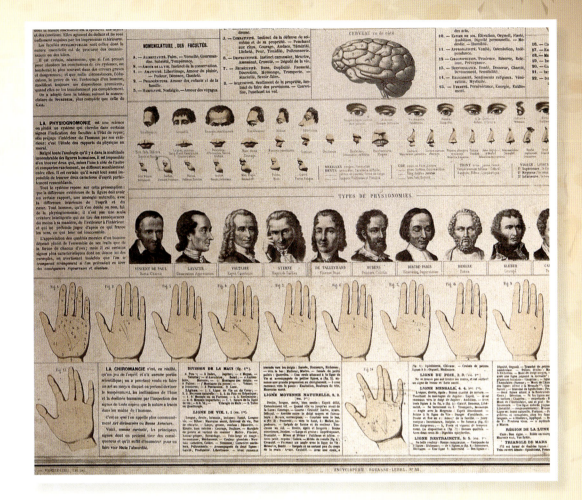

Chirognomie, or in English "chirognomy," from the Greek for "hand understanding."

What is interesting about D'Arpentigny's book is that he never mentions the lines of the palm; rather, he focuses on the significance of finger length, fingertips, joints, and hand shape, and describes how the physiology of the hand relates to individual personality. It is possible that D'Arpentigny wanted to distance himself from the Roma people who introduced him to the practice of reading palms, wanting to present a more "scientific" commentary.

La Chirognomie signaled a renewal of interest in the art of studying hands. His work endures as a foundation today.

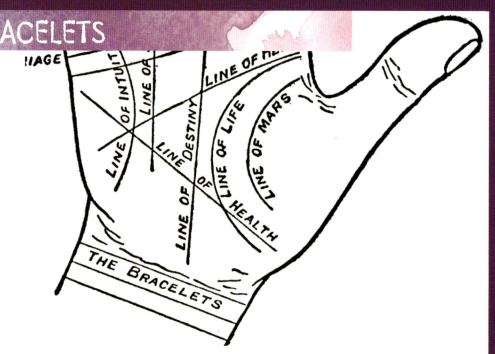

The illustration labels: IIAGE, LINE OF INTUIT, LINE OF, LINE OF H—, LINE OF MARS, LINE OF DESTINY, LINE OF LIFE, LINE OF, LINE OF HEALTH, THE BRACELETS

RINGS OF HISTORY

The bracelets, or rascettes, are rings around the wrist. When Rosa Baughan was researching and writing about palmistry, western palm readers almost all repeated the idea that the bracelets represented some number of years of life.

Whether that number was 25 or 30 or something else, each bracelet counted toward life span, and three bracelets together constituted a "magic bracelet." Because of this purported link, the bracelets are only second perhaps to the life line for something outsiders always ask about palmistry: "I've heard these rings each mean 25 years of life, is that right?"

Today, we say no. The truth is that most people have three complete bracelets or some combination of partial bracelets that add up to three.

ROBUST CONSTITUTION

If we toss out this idea that the bracelets measure our

life span, we can instead look at them as indicators of someone's overall constitution, meaning their collection of factors of wellness.

Most people have three complete bracelets, and most people are healthy. The one health link that modern palmists still point to is that a bracelet stretching up toward the wrist means the person may have reproductive challenges.

The term constitution is interesting, implying that health is a collection of balanced parts, like the constituents of a congressional district or the collection of articles and amendments that make up a nation's constitution.

In Henry David Thoreau's journals of his life's pursuit of some higher meaning, he often mentioned his daily constitutional—a term referring to a walk, but with the added suggestion that this walk helps balance one's health and its constituent parts. A sound mind is worth several bracelets at least, and Thoreau knew it.

"Mr. Garvace was a short stout man, with that air of modest pride that so often goes with corpulence, choleric and decisive in manner, and with hands that looked like bunches of fingers."
— H.G. Wells

DRAGON'S TAIL

In Hindu palmistry, the arched top bracelet helps to form the mount of dragon's tail. The neutral area in the center of the palm, usually called the plain of Mars in western palmistry, forms the dragon's head. The mount of dragon's tail works in concert with the destiny line, and its position low on the hand means palmists use it to study the early childhood. The old Hindu texts say the mount of dragon's tail affects a child's future success, because a weak mount can indicate a financially struggling family that can destabilize a child's prospects. Rosa Baughan reiterates this a bit, writing in her book that hands with the triple "magic" bracelet are lucky, "indicating long life, health and riches."

MOUNT OF NEPTUNE

Western palmists sometimes categorize the mount of dragon's tail as the mount of Neptune. Because it's nestled between the mount of Luna and the mount of Venus, the mount of Neptune can embody the juncture of both qualities. Venus is hands on, passionate, and caring, while the moon is intuitive, reflective, and influential. With those poles in mind, the mount of Neptune links them in the same spirit as Mercury, the messenger, by weaving the different signals together into one high-quality stream of thought. Strong mounts of Neptune can be great consultants, public speakers, or project managers.

The mount of Neptune can also host an unusual feature of the fingerprint-like ridges that really cover the whole surface of our fingers and palms. The loop of inspiration, also known as the loop of empathy, marks the mount of Neptune of someone who is moved in a powerful way by meaningful works of art or other kinds of events.

There's a technical term for someone who feels faint or sick in the face of great beauty, named Stendhal syndrome after an afflicted soldier in Napoleon Bonaparte's army. Stendhal's real name was Marie-Henri Beyle, and he was a prolific writer of fiction and nonfiction. Critics note how Stendhal's work toed the line between reality and the dreamy flights of fancy of Romanticism, making him, ostensibly, an archetypal mount of Neptune.

Research on Stendhal syndrome often includes the German poet Rainer Maria Rilke's famous line: "Denn das Schöne ist nichts als des Schrecklichen Anfang." *Because beauty is nothing but the beginning of the terrible.* For the neptunian personality, the strong visceral reaction to the beautiful or awe-inspiring can be terrible indeed.

MOUNT OF NEPTUNE

THE SUN
SATURN
JUPITER
MERCURY
MARS POSITIVE
MARS NEGATIVE
THE MOON
VENUS LOVE

TRAVEL LINES

TRAVEL LINES

Everyone has bracelets, but not everyone has the related feature known as the travel lines. These begin on the topmost bracelet and wend upward onto the mount of the moon. The lunar archetype at its best is a voracious traveler (or armchair traveler!) who loves to see new things and fit them into the lunarian's complex vision of the world.

If this person is interested in traveling alone, as the solitary lunarian is apt to be, their travels may lead them to meet new people who end up being important in their lives. Baughan describes these as indicated by longer travel lines that may reach as far as the heart or head line.

The callous palms of the laborer are conversant with finer tissues of self-respect and heroism, whose touch thrills the heart, than the languid fingers of idleness."
— Henry David Thoreau

THE THUMB

Having an opposable thumb, meaning one we can use together with our fingers to pinch, grab, and manipulate items, makes humans unusual.

Very few species have opposable thumbs at all, and fewer still have thumbs as long as ours. Human thumbs are articulated with three joints, and they're about the same length as the rest of our fingers. We are special because of our articulate thumbs.

At the same time, our thumbs aren't unique in other ways. Honestly, very few things about humans are unique instead of just unusual or contextually important. Our thumbs are more talented and nimble than those of even our close exigent ancestors, but there's no X factor—all the elements of our thumbs, like muscles, are the same component parts as in other great apes.

In a way, the thumb is symbolic of what makes palmistry so interesting. Sure, the human thumb is assembled from the same biological warehouse as the similar thumbs of other species. Our brains and bodies are recognizable as belonging to the same group of great apes, even with our evolutionary step forward. We still experience fight, flight, or freeze and other instinctive animal feelings.

But none of this flat scientific information explains why humans make the most complex music, build ships to explore outer space, and work together in advanced social systems. We are greater than the sum of our individual parts, exemplified by our thumbs. It turns out there really is an X factor, and the nature of it remains a mystery. On top of that, we still must contend with our animal instincts.

SIZE OF THE THUMB

We measure the thumb in comparison to the rest of the hand and fingers. Hold your thumb straight up with your hand flat. If your thumb falls about halfway up the bottom third of the Jupiter finger, this is the average or neutral length. Long thumbs and short thumbs each bring suggested qualities, but the medium thumb brings the two together with pleasing harmony. The variation in thumbs can be down to just a few sixteenths of an inch, so a "short thumb" and a "big thumb" will be exactly as functional—our distinction here is all spiritual.

BIG THUMBS UP

Think of the thumb as a reservoir for pragmatism and determination. The large thumb overshadows the mount of Venus where it begins and reaches instead for the Jupiter finger. If it's indeed a silo for stick-to-itness, more volume means more capacity to take adversity in stride and keep working toward long-term goals and ambitions.

Most of us know some version of the ancient parable of the elephant and the blind men: with palmistry, our hands are the elephants, and we must be careful not to mistake one wrinkle or outcropping for the whole thing. The thumb can be linked with Venus to some extent, but its overall identity is malleable.

Someone can "stick to it" toward a goal that causes harm to others, and it's important to consider all the features of the hand together. The best way to keep this idea in mind is to think of the large thumb as an amplifier: whatever is already going on, this thumb will make it louder.

THE MEDIUM THUMB

If the large thumb is an amplifier, the medium or average-size thumb is a ballast to comfortably balance the rest of the hand. People with medium thumbs may still have times of strong drive toward ambitious goals, it just isn't one of their defining qualities. Like we'll see in a minute with short thumbs, medium thumbs may still have times of strong affinity for creativity, sensuality, and aesthetics.

While some medium thumbs will oscillate between these two groups, others will have a more overall even keel that strikes a smoother balance. These people can find success in roles where their ability to see everyone's perspectives is valued. If they have a nice mount of Neptune, Mercury finger, or even a Saturn finger leaning into the Jupiter finger, they might be unstoppable at something like motivational speaking, life coaching, or leading group counseling sessions.

THE SHORT THUMB

We find a short thumb on the hand of a true aesthete, someone who, depending on their other hand features, could be anything from a cashmere-wrapped homebody to an extraordinary bon vivant.

With so much less volume, their thumbs don't act as a ballast or an amplifier but rather as a natural extension of the mount of Venus. As with the long thumb, there are potential downsides to the short thumb. With so much less emphasis on the persistence of the long thumb, short thumbs can end up acting flighty or pursuing their aesthetic and sensory goals over everything else.

If you know a very talented creator who's also a social butterfly, they might have a short thumb that leads them to act a little capricious with RSVPs or other commitments.

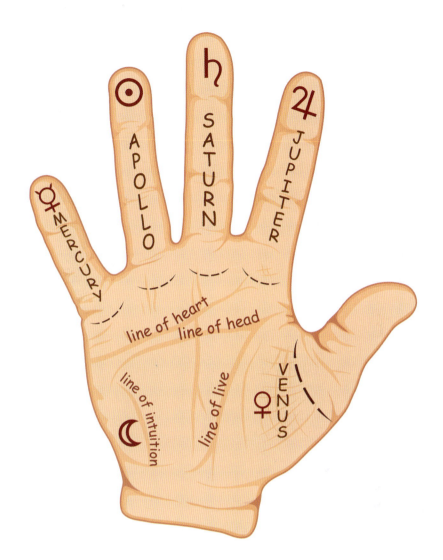

So what's the ideal length for the thumb? This varies so much depending on the person's overall temperament, strengths, and weaknesses. If the long thumb complements a hand marked by signs of stubbornness and narrow thinking, we could be dealing with a real boor. A short thumb on a water hand whose head line is chained with islands could indicate someone whose wonderful creativity comes in short spurts before they're too tired, but the work they made in that short time could be astonishing.

THE THUMB

SECTIONS OF THE THUMB

The webbing of the thumb can partly hide that the thumb has three sections just like the other fingers. Because the very bottom-most section overlaps the mount of Venus, most palmists don't consider it separately. Of the two discrete sections, the top one represents willpower, individuality, and strength of purpose. The bottom section represents reason, logic, and the methodical side of thinking. For most people, the two sections are roughly the same length, showing the idea of balance between strength of will and methodical reasoning.

Each section's qualities are heightened or lessened by the relative length of the section, and this harmonizes with the whole thumb's relative length as well. If the top section of the thumb is slightly shorter than the bottom section, this represents the most common configuration and shows that reasoning is a little stronger than the will. But if the top section is much shorter than the bottom or vice versa, that indicates an imbalance in traits that can affect thinking and personality.

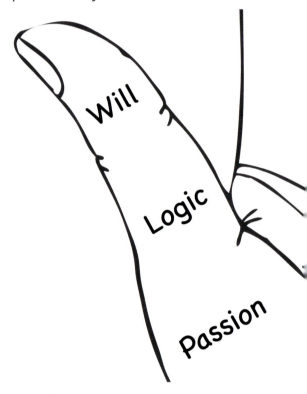

The unseen third section of the thumb, the one that lies beneath the mount of Venus, makes an emotional base for the rest of the thumb.

Because of this, the logic section of the thumb is really important. This section links the emotional mount of Venus and the strength of will of the tip of the thumb, making it a mediator between two powerful forces. If the logical bottom section is short, it can't be a strong and equal mediator.

Traditional palmists say a narrow bottom section indicates more grace and tact, especially if it's fairly long compared to the top section of the thumb.

The top section of the thumb can vary widely in shape, and it represents a kind of lightning rod or antenna not just for strength of will but for the energy and inspiration to pursue what the will indicates. And it doesn't stop there— the thumb's tip is unique and speaks to the whole personality in a way other individual fingertips do not, the same way the thumb overall occupies a "spokesperson" place the other individual fingers do not.

A broader bottom section can point to a more straightforward or even blunt personality, although it can be balanced with the other sections of the thumb and mitigated. Sometimes the bottom section is so narrow that its sides appear concave. This person may be very diplomatic and genuine, interested in mediating and with significant talent for it. At the same time, they may be somewhat manipulative, able to pull social strings in a machiavellian way.

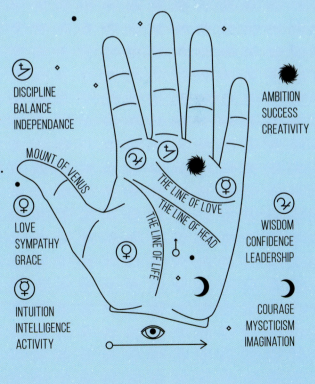

DISCIPLINE
BALANCE
INDEPENDANCE

AMBITION
SUCCESS
CREATIVITY

MOUNT OF VENUS

THE LINE OF LOVE

THE LINE OF HEAD

THE LINE OF LIFE

LOVE
SYMPATHY
GRACE

WISDOM
CONFIDENCE
LEADERSHIP

INTUITION
INTELLIGENCE
ACTIVITY

COURAGE
MYSCTICISM
IMAGINATION

If the thumb tip is very pointed, this is considered extreme, channeling an otherworldly will so powerful that this person often has their head completely in the clouds and out of any practical everyday concerns.

A true pointed thumb is rare, but the next shape, a gentler point referred to as a conical thumb, is both more common and more grounded in reality. Energy flow is still tapered and focused, just not to a degree that totally crowds out the susurration of the

mundane. Rather than live in a world completely of their own, conical thumbs have ideas and perspectives that remain open and responsive to the ideas and feelings of others. They feel strongly but are not unreachable or unchangeable.

A conical thumb tip can also range from narrower to wider, depending on the angle of the sloping sides and the relative width of the very tip of the cone. A wider cone shaped more like a trapezoid will have less of that focused energy than more of a triangle.

If the tip of the thumb is even and squared off with little or no taper to the tip, these folks are more grounded and less tuned in with the creative and spiritual. They may prefer to lead workgroups rather than serve as the brainstormers or creators on those teams. They may even be dynamic, creative thinkers within the realms they feel comfortable in, helping to streamline systems.

The opposite extreme of the pointed thumb is so wide and squared off that the thumb's tip is its widest point. The tip flares from the middle joint, creating both an abundance of will and a closed-off pathway to higher energy. In fact, people with a flared and blunt thumb may be dedicated to their own ways of life with an almost spiritual level of devotion and unwavering commitment.

Despite an important-sounding name, the health line is considered a lesser line, and palmists say just half of people have one or both health lines.

Using palmistry to predict specifics of physical health and well being is an old-fashioned form of fortune-telling that verges on the same old territory as phrenology, and being able bodied doesn't indicate anything about someone's mind, personality, or capacity for happiness.

The health line is also called the Mercury line and the hepatica, both of which speak to the well meaning but misguided approach to health and wellness in ancient times. In the 21st century, we understand that the human body has related systems of organs and tissues that keep the body in what scientists call homeostasis, meaning "operating within normal parameters."

But for much of the 2,000 years before that discovery, scientists

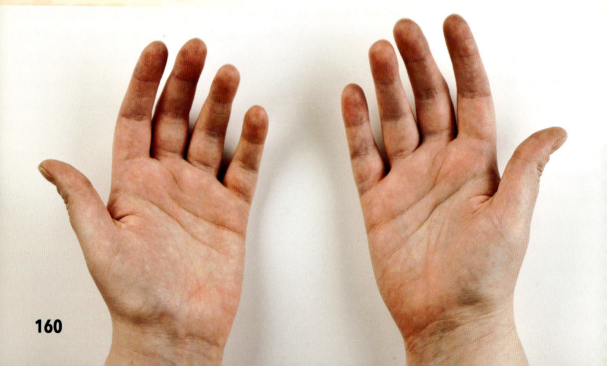

made educated guesses about what happened inside the body. In these scientists's theory of overall health, the human body had four fluids, or humors: blood, yellow bile, black bile, and phlegm.

They assigned blood to the liver, yellow and black bile to the gallbladder and spleen, and phlegm to the lungs. We still use words like melancholy (meaning, literally, "black fluid"), phlegmatic, and sanguine ("related to blood") that originate in the theory that these fluids affect our personalities, especially when they fall out of balance and disrupt our heatlh.

The theory of four humors sounds so archaic to our 21st-century ears, but western physicians used humorism as a guiding principle for two thousand years. Other sciences had similar growing pains!

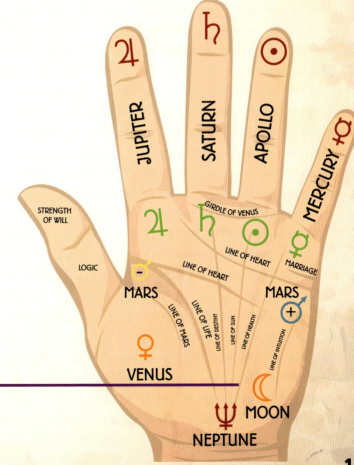

HEALTH LINE

To be sanguine, the theory goes, was to be lively, agreeable, and sociably warm. The descriptors associated with blood were moist and warm, which makes sense, since blood is what keeps our bodies alive instead of cold and dry.

Rather than identify the heart as the center of the circulatory system that powers the body, these ancient scientists associated blood with the liver, which we now know is just a pitstop where blood is filtered and cleaned. The blood technically comes from inside our bones, and it is circulated by our blood vessels and the pumping of the heart.

But as a result of all these related misunderstandings, the word hepatica, which means "of the liver," was interchangeably used to describe overall

physical health. In some older palmistry texts, the line representing health is called the liver line. Many other forms of divination have a corresponding health aspect of their own that was originally named for the liver. Terms like "lily livered," which dates back to the turn of the 17th century, use a hale and hearty liver as an emblem for

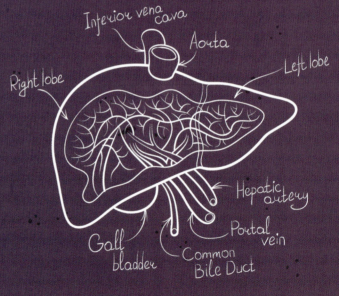

Inferior vena cava
Aorta
Right lobe
Left lobe
Hepatic artery
Gall bladder
Common Bile Duct
Portal vein

the life-giving healthfulness and strength of blood.

The liver, health, or Mercury line runs in a diagonal from beneath the mount of Venus toward the heart line's source at the pinky edge of the palm. It's called the Mercury line because it ends close to or on the edge of the Mercury mount.

Palmists's opinions on the Mercury line vary a bit, seeming to hinge on whether someone enjoys a gamble. If there's no Mercury line, there can be no bad interpretation made of the Mercury line. Some palmists say it's flat-out better not to have

this line at all and avoid the risk altogether. A clear, consistent Mercury line is said to indicate good overall physical wellness. But those with no Mercury line are just as physically well.

The only poor form of Mercury line is one which is dashed, faint, or marked with islands and braiding. As with other lines, short parallel "helper lines" or rectangular sets of marks that enclose places on the Mercury line are thought to show protection.

There's a special case where someone's palm has no destiny line but does have a health line. The celestial bodies at play mean the Mercury qualities of the health line can pick up some of the slack created by the absent Saturn line, substituting Mercury's more frenetic and communicative cleverness for the more circumspect wisdom-seeking of Saturn. It's not a perfect one-to-one exchange, but everything on the hand is about finding balance in a well rounded life.

JUPITER
SATURN
APOLLO
MERCURY

STRENGTH OF WILL
GIRDLE OF VENUS
LINE OF HEART
LOGIC
LINE OF HEART
MARRIAGE
MARS
MARS
LINE OF LIFE
LINE OF MARS
LINE OF DESTINY
LINE OF SUN
LINE OF HEALTH
LINE OF INTUITION
VENUS
MOON
NEPTUNE
BRACELETS OF LIFE

"But every modern god will now extend
His vast prerogative as far as Jove.
To rage, to lust, to write to, to commend,
All is the purlieu of the god of love."
— John Donne, "Love's Deity"

At the very beginning of this book, we went over each finger's identity and history as a cursory introduction to finger shape, size, and arrangement. The Jupiter finger is the pointer or index finger, used for all of recorded history as a way at least some people on Earth were showing each other where to look. It even shows up in print, beginning with hand-illustrated versions nearly 400 years before the invention of the printing press.

The terms "index finger" and "pointer finger" are redundant in a sense, because the Latin word *index* already means both the first finger and the idea of something that's pointing, leading to other related words like *indicate*. A pointer dog or idioms like "get to the point" come from this same origin. In the United States, our obscene gesture using the middle finger may be more emphatic, but to point with the Jupiter finger is far older and more common.

On the ceiling of the Sistine Chapel, Michelangelo shows God imbuing Adam with life by reaching his strong index finger toward Adam. Adam's hand is held limply—he is not yet truly alive, and his arm is braced against his leg for support—but his index finger is also slightly outstretched.

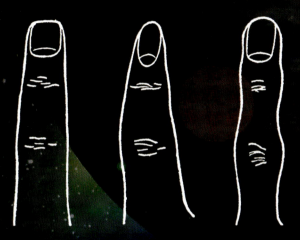

FINGER FEATURES

From this prevalence, it's easy to see why the forefinger represents Jupiter's influence, the same way the solar system's largest planet dominates our imagination with its size and power. The Jupiter finger and the mount beneath it speak to our ability to lead, visualize grand plans, and be ambitious when setting goals. At the same time, the Jupiter features hopefully show us how to be magnanimous and kind as we pursue our goals. As with the tip of the thumb, the fingertip shape represents how much energy is powering the qualities of each finger, and how receptive this person is to higher or more far-out ideas. If the Jupiter finger has a tapered tip, this person may want to make their grand plans for a religious or spiritual organization or spend their time advocating for a philosophical idea that could help others. With a more square or even flared tip, their projects may be more grounded in the everyday, but these folks will still have big goals and be able to captivate a room with their presence.

JUPITER FINGER

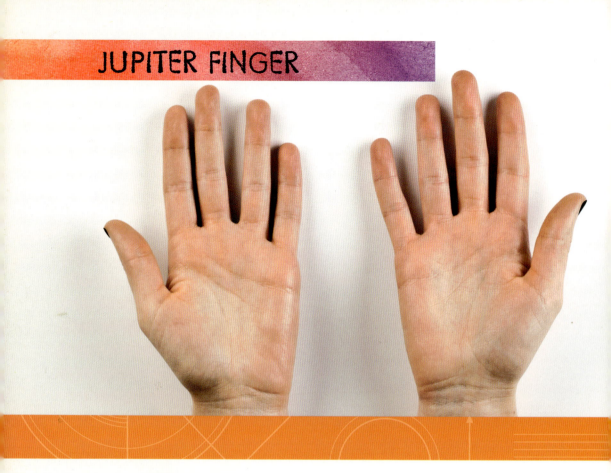

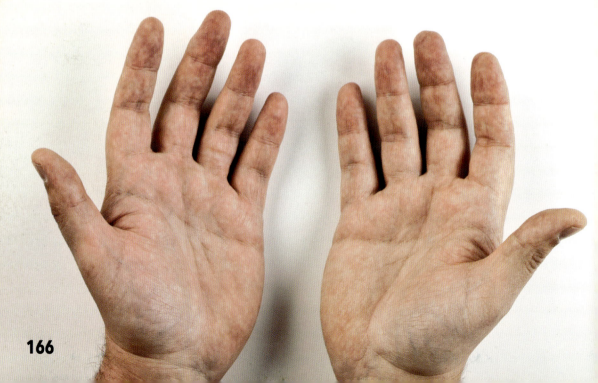

THE LONG AND SHORT

On the abstract "ideal hand," the Jupiter finger is the same length as the Apollo, or ring, finger. When this is the case, the two influences balance each other and lead to harmony in one's goals and projects. Apollo's creativity and spirit of earthly indulgence are a natural complement to Jupiter's largeness of purpose.

If the Jupiter finger is especially long compared with the Apollo finger, this can indicate someone who struggles to balance their dogged pursuit of goals with the Apollo qualities that allow us to stop and smell—or sketch—the roses.

An unchecked Jupiter influence can lead to burnout, because even the most dedicated and inspired worker or leader must take breaks and let their mind rest sometimes. If the Apollo finger isn't there as a balance, the strong Jupiter can look to others to help them know when to pause and ask for help.

What if the Jupiter finger is short overall or has one especially short section? These folks can still work hard and be capable leaders, but their success will be in more workaday roles rather than as decisionmakers or in highly visible positions.

Their appeal can be subtle, too. They could be the member of their team to whom others naturally confide and ask for advice: not technically above anyone else in pay or job, but with qualities that draw positive attention and respect.

This is especially true if the mount of Jupiter is high, firm, and unmarked, with a position more below the Jupiter finger than the neighboring Saturn finger. A short Jupiter finger is largely offset by a strong Jupiter mount, the same way a long, elegant Jupiter finger could be mitigated by a weak or overly saturnine-leaning Jupiter mount.

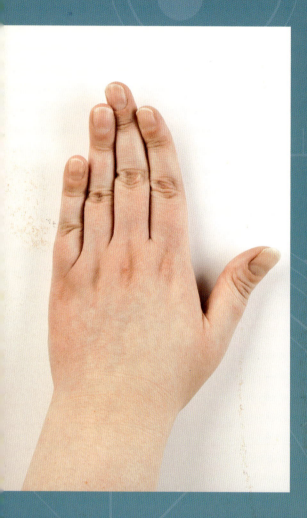

LEANING IN

In our discussion of whether fingers are straight or leaning, we talked a bit about how a leaning finger is influenced by the direction where it leans. If the Jupiter finger leans toward the Saturn, this can show that Jupiter is sending its energy and enlivening force into the Saturn finger. If the opposite is true instead, and the Saturn finger leans toward a straighter Jupiter finger, this person's ambitions and plans may be more grounded because of Saturn's tendency toward caution and prudence. Too much Saturn could impede Jupiter, leading to moroseness instead of energy and pessimism instead of optimism.

MAKING CONNECTIONS

Buddhism and Hinduism have some shared symbology, which includes sacred hand poses called mudras. Each finger has an element that, when joined in a circle with the thumb, creates a channel for that element's energy.

The Jupiter finger in western palmistry is the air element in this system of mudras, and the circle of Jupiter finger and thumb forms a connection that symbolizes the link between one mind and many minds. In this sense, the mudra harmonizes with our understanding of Jupiter's potential for leadership and innovation that helps others.

MOUNT UP

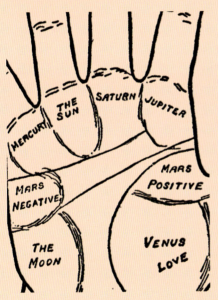

The Jupiter mount is often the largest and most visible mount on the palm, reflecting Jupiter's outsize role in the pantheon of gods, the solar system, and on the hand. The simplest Jupiter mount is one which is clear, raised, and consistently firm, showing a dominant Jupiter type that is uncomplicated by marks. Different arrangements of faint or strong lines, including the X shapes or asterisks formed by those lines, mean different things for the hand's Jupiter influence.

A single line may be good or bad depending on its arrangement. In general, one line crossing the mount vertically is thought of as a continuation of that finger, magnifying its effect by adding length. Faint lines that overlap like cross-hatching can show that someone is either stifling their jovian nature or that their life circumstances are stifling it for them. An X formed by two lines is considered a bad sign, but a star formed by three lines is considered a good sign. Look closely and think about what each marking might indicate in relation to Jupiter's traits.

RUNIC PALMISTRY

Although the origins of palm reading seem to point to southern and eastern Asia, the most widely practiced form of palmistry today, called "classical" palmistry, is based on ancient Roman and Greek belief systems.

The reasons for this are unclear, but it is believed that during the time of Alexander the Great and Julius Caesar, the art of palmistry was extremely popular in Greece and Rome, where people often looked to the skies—to the stars and astrology—for answers and comfort. As a result, palmistry is intertwined with the sky.

A HANDY REFERENCE

In fact, many felt that human fate was determined by the stars; and as hands were said to provide a map of human fate, it stands to reason that the lines and other characteristics of the hand would reflect the

stars and planets in the sky. Around the world, different groups scrutinized the stars, their calendars, omens found in the changing daily weather, and more. Today, each area of the hand is associated with a different god or goddess, reflecting the ancient historical significance of the practice.

Ancient peoples were familiar with the qualities that each of these gods and goddesses was said to possess, and they assigned the same qualities to the areas on the hand the deities were said to represent.

The fingers and the mounts below each one are represented by Mercury, Apollo, Saturn, and Jupiter. Jupiter, which is represented by the index finger and the mount underneath it, was said to be the leader of the gods; the Jupiter area of the hand is said to reflect leadership ability and self-confidence—or a lack thereof.

RUNIC PALMISTRY

A RUNE OF ONE'S OWN

But classical palmistry is not the only method for uncovering the attributes of the hands that has developed throughout centuries. Another method, called runic palmistry, stems from Norse mythology. As the mythology goes, a great tree called Yggdrasil stands at the center of the Norse universe, cradling the world of Asgard in its branches (yes, Marvel movie fans—the same Asgard that houses Chris Hemsworth's Thor). The tree grows out of the Well of Urd, a pool that contains some of the most powerful beings in the universe.

These beings shape fate by carving runes—symbols that create consequential, world-shaping forces—into the tree. Runes live on today as a major part of fantasy literature and games, including imbuing Marvel's version of Thor with magical powers. Even today, Bluetooth technology is named for a medieval Scandinavian king, and its ubiquitous logo is made from runes.

SHAPES IN THE HAND

In runic palmistry's origin story, Odin, the ruler of Asgard, saw the power held by the beings in the Well of Urd and sought it for himself. To do so, he pierced himself with his own spear to a branch of Yggdrasil, where he hung for nine days. Finally, he finally began to see the runes within the Well of Urd, and was gifted with the knowledge of how to use the symbols to vanquish enemies and protect his people.

Runic palmistry believes that the same symbols that Odin searched for are now found within the palm of the hand. And just like in classical palmistry, runic palmistry assigns different gods to different areas of the hand. Odin—the leader of the gods—is representative of the index finger, just as the leader of the Roman gods, Jupiter, represents the index finger in classical palmistry.

SATURN FINGER

For most people, the Saturn or middle finger is the longest finger. It's interesting that Jupiter, the leader, is necessarily balanced with the Apollo finger while the Saturn finger is the tallest, the centermost, and unchecked by a natural counterpart. With its celestial influence from both a complex planet and an elder god, Saturn represents the wisdom of the ages and the idea that everything averages out over a long enough period of time. But with that long view comes the potential for darkness, sadness, and existential dread.

A TITAN OF MALEFICENCE

TITAN
Saturn

The ancient god Saturn embodies the same sense of ambivalence and chaos as the astrological and chiromantic aspect of Saturn. Originally, Saturn was the Greek titan Cronus, born of the generation between the primordial deities like Gaia and the more popular pantheon led by Zeus. In Greek myth, Cronus stopped at nothing to attain and hold onto power, including castrating and overthrowing his father Uranus and planning to consume any children he fathered. But like his later earthly carbon copy Oedipus, his plan to subvert his destiny backfired in a spectacular way.

Cronus would seem like a tragic hero if he hadn't been such a huge jerk, but the Greeks thought of him more like a cautionary tale that fit with the flawed personalities of the other titans. He ruled mythical ancient Greece during the time that coined the term Golden Age, when people naturally lived long, peaceful lives while sampling the abundance of the land around them. In a way, it's like the portion of Genesis when figures like Methuselah are described as living for hundreds of years, and related ideas from other belief systems around the world.

SATURN

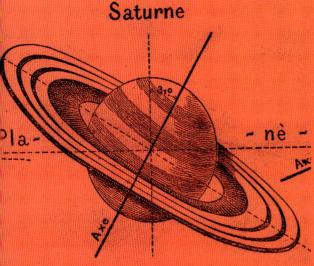

Saturne

In embracing Cronus's legacy as the ruler of the prototypical Golden Age, the Romans happily overlooked or just deemphasized the titan's paranoia and attempted filial cannibalism. Saturn's separate Roman name has helped keep the legacies separate, too: the god of harvest and abundance gives his name to a planet with thousands of rings and over 60 moons, including one named Titan. Because of this emblematic planet, Saturn is a car manufacturer, a major science fiction award, a Sailor Moon character, and a beloved Sega console.

ROMAN HOLIDAY

During this time of not just prosperity but omnivalent peace, Cronus was never challenged. But his leadership was born of betrayal and died in betrayal as well, and Cronus was paranoid, cruel, and capricious. In Greece, he was portrayed holding the curved blade he'd used to dethrone his father. But the Romans embraced Cronus, whom they adapted as Saturn. The curved blade became the scythe of a farmer, and Saturn became the god of the harvest.

On the other hand, Cronus is nowhere to be found in popular culture. Almost everything named Kronos, which does look like a more accurate Greek spelling, is actually about Chronos, the proto-god responsible for moving time forward. Ancient Greek spirituality wasn't unified, and the vast majority of communication was oral, not written. Chronos and Cronus grew together over time like trees attempting to share the same space.

When scientists or writers do name things for Cronus, not Chronos, it's because of a real or anthropomorphized bad behavior. In 2017, scientists at Princeton named a star Kronos after theorizing that it somehow consumed its own planets, giving it an unusually wide selection of elements in its mass. Like a cartoon character, star Kronos is claiming it didn't eat Tweety Bird, but is nonetheless belching out feathers.

THE COMBINED SATURN

In palmistry, the Saturn we discuss is almost entirely the Roman take, combining the good parts of Cronus with some of the time, patience, and wisdom of Chronos. Saturn types are often quiet and industrious, as is reflected in the qualities of a good destiny line. They're bright, hardworking, and often a bit distant. This can be out of true introversion or because they prefer to live in the world of the mind.

For a darker Saturn type, the same distance could speak to sadness or isolation. Dark Saturns can embody some of the true Cronus qualities like paranoia and cynicism. They're smart enough to spin big theories, but may be too absorbed in minutiae to really understand that those theories are wild or overly pessimistic. Cronus ruled over the most peaceful and ideal age in ancient Greek legend, but he was still so afraid of the inevitable passage of time and progress that he took outlandish and ineffective steps to try to stop it.

FINGER FEATURES

The Saturn finger's height over the rest of the fingers speaks to its tendency toward solitude. If the fingertip is more tapered and narrow, solitude may even tip into full-blown misanthropy, even if it's of an upbeat nature. This person could still be fun to spend time with but may prove to be an unreliable friend. They could also be a sharp and observant critic. A more square tip on the Saturn finger can indicate someone whose intelligence is more patient and grounded but who probably will not tip into melancholy or overly sharp criticism. The square tip is fairly neutral.

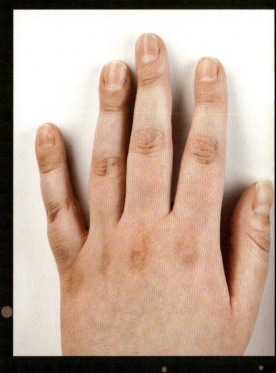

If the fingertip is flared, or spatulate, this person is most susceptible to Saturn's gloomier qualities. This may mean lashing out at others, but it's more likely a quiet and enduring melancholy. Depending on the rest of the hand, these folks may still find contentedness by making art that mitigates their sadness, or even by pursuing careers that involve helping themselves and others prepare for the worst in order to reduce harm. If the Saturn finger has an especially padded tip, this can add to the melancholy. It can also help these Saturns better express their sadness in order to process it in healthy ways.

SATURN FINGER

THE LONG AND SHORT

With no similar finger to compare, the Saturn finger is in a category of its own. If the Saturn finger is noticeably long even by the usual standard, this often means someone is even more solitary by nature. Combined with a strong Luna mount on a water hand, this person could be a dreamy and artistic scholar who likes to think through complex problems but not collaborate.

The solitary pursuit of wisdom is embodied by so-called "outsider" scientists who often can't succeed in academic settings even if they have access to them. Famous outsider mathematician Srinivasa Ramanujan dropped out of college twice and did subsistence clerical work in southern India. He only lived to be 32, but in that short time he wrote down nearly 4,000 mathematical discoveries that have almost all been proven correct since his death in 1920. Ramanujan was motivated to study and imagine mathematical ideas by his religious beliefs, aligning him with humankind's long history of sacred study of math, science, letters, and numbers.

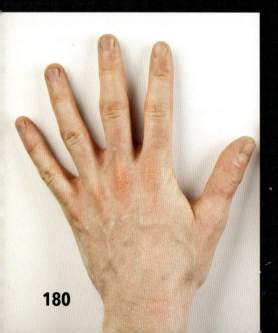

If the Saturn finger is shorter and therefore closer to the Jupiter and Apollo fingers, this doesn't indicate closer social ties so much as a confusion of social responsibilities. This person may be careless or feckless in addition to being solitary. When it comes to the length of the Saturn finger, an average, unremarkable length is best—no news is good news.

LEANING IN

When it comes to leans, the Saturn finger has an unwieldy amount of influence. If the Jupiter or Apollo fingers lean toward Saturn, they imbue Saturn with their qualities, adding interest if not always in a good way. But if Saturn leans toward Jupiter or Apollo, it dampens their qualities while adding none of its own. That characterization is a bit misleading, because Saturn does add its tendency toward stifling or melancholy, which has the effect of reducing the energy and potency of its neighbors. Adding a negative quality is the same as subtracting a good one in this case.

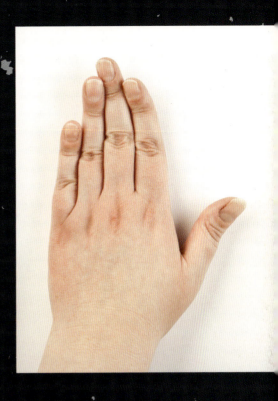

MAKING CONNECTIONS

The middle finger represents the element of connection in the sacred hand geometries of Hindu and Buddhist mudras. Bringing the thumb and middle finger together creates a grounding pose that encourages follow-through and patience. Again we see how different world traditions notice and value similar qualities in their studies of shared body features. The Chronos influence on the Saturn finger gives it a timeless feeling that pairs well with meditative use of mudras.

SATURN
MOUNT

LUNA
MOUNT

MOUNT UP

As with the Saturn finger, the Saturn mount is another case where unremarkability or absence is the best option. Saturn's qualities are balanced so delicately that adding the good aspects brings an uncommonly high risk of adding the bad aspects as well. This is more true in the mount than in the Saturn finger, because the average person's Saturn mount is genuinely flat. If the flat area is wider, pushing other mounts further away, this reflects Saturn's preference for solitude.

Because most Saturn mounts are flat, even a little bit of dimension really amps up the influence of Saturn. An encroaching Jupiter or Apollo mount can influence Saturn, but the tallest and most independent finger is simply not very suggestible. The destiny line may extend up into the area created where a mount of Saturn would be, and if so, this is considered a good sign. There can also be a discrete vertical line that nonetheless merges with the destiny line. Either one indicates a focus and energizing of positive Saturn qualities.

If the destiny line loosely describes the path of our lives, its end near or on the mount of Saturn shows the later part of life. Again, we see the influence of Chronos, allowing the passage of time to make our good qualities better and our bad qualities even worse. Especially for Saturn, growing old can come with drastically polarized results. A choleric Saturn may grow much moreso in old age, especially if their nature is critical and anxious. Health problems caused by depression or ongoing stress can continue to drag their mood down. But an aging Saturn may also learn to relax, let go of some of their worries, and let other people help them a bit more. The later part of life could turn out to be a Saturn's happiest time period.

While the vertical line is a good sign, a strong horizontal line across this mount is a bad sign. Instead of an antenna, this line acts as a stopper and a spoiler. Energy attempting to travel through is pushed backward or squashed out toward nearby features, throwing them out of balance while starving other areas.

DESTINY LINE

APOLLO FINGER

Because of the western tradition of the wedding ring, the Apollo or ring finger is arguably the most famous of the bunch. And as global connectivity continues to grow, the wedding ring only gets more and more popular in China and other eastern countries where it was never a tradition. The purported reason we put our wedding rings on the Apollo finger goes back hundreds of years to another charming but totally incorrect medical theory.

VENA AMORIS

Today, we've fully documented the circulatory system that powers the human body. All of our extremities are traced through with blood vessels that branch into finer and finer strands to reach to our fingertips and toes. But in Renaissance Europe and perhaps before, they started to put wedding rings on the Apollo finger because they believed it held a vein that connected directly to the heart. Of course, there's no such vein. That hasn't changed the western world's almost unvarying preference for the wedding ring finger in the centuries since.

The Venus mount on the palm is considered the "lover," but the Apollo finger is also a good choice for lore about the heart. Apollo represents not romantic love but love for art, poetry, and music. Strong Apollo types are charismatic or even magnetic, and most palmistry texts describe too much Apollo influence as leading to flightiness, as with social butterflies who make shallow commitments as they pursue society goals.

THE SUN ALWAYS RISES

But Apollo, the Greek god of the sun, is never flighty. He's the patron god of animal husbandry, the same way Cronus is the god of the harvest of crops. In the contemporary writings of ancient Greeks, Apollo oversaw the Muses, and some may have even been his daughters. Because of this, Apollo is implied to be the patron of the arts. The word paean, meaning a song of praise, originates with one of Apollo's many names: Apollo Paean, the Apollo of healing. Over time, one specific song of thanksgiving became, like Kleenex, the household term for any song of thanksgiving.

And because it was an Apollonian temple that housed the Oracle at Delphi—a real person and place, made immortal when Sophocles wrote her as delivering a prophecy to Oedipus Rex—Apollo is also the god of prophecies. All this, and Apollo is also literally the sun, the largest and most powerful celestial body in our solar system. The mount of Venus may stand for romantic love, but Apollo is steadfast, faithful, beautiful, and warm.

APOLLO FINGER

FINGER FEATURES

The Apollo finger should be roughly the same length as the Jupiter finger, indicating a balance between the lovingkindness of Apollo and the ambition of Jupiter. Both should be within about a fingernail's length of Saturn, showing that Saturn is still surrounded by positive influences. But the interplay between Jupiter and Apollo mirrors an idea introduced by the Nihilist philosopher Friedrich Nietzsche, who posited Apollo and his brother Dionysus as opposites that must always be in conflict.

The same way Saturn needs both Jupiter and Apollo, Jupiter and Apollo need each other in order to create a harmonious life. The balance will tilt back and forth from day to day, but these changes will disappear in the long view of time. If Apollo has a more tapered fingertip, this person's sense of artistry may aim toward the sublime and transcendent, with religious work or intensely emotional abstract work. A wider fingertip could indicate creation and stewardship of organizations with creative goals.

JUPITER

SATURN

APOLLO

MERCURY

STRENGTH OF WILL

GIRDLE OF VENUS

LINE OF HEART

LOGIC

LINE OF HEART

MARRIAGE

MARS

MARS

LINE OF MARS

LINE OF LIFE

LINE OF DESTINY

LINE OF SUN

LINE OF HEALTH

LINE OF INTUITION

VENUS

MOON

NEPTUNE

BRACELETS OF LIFE

THE LONG AND SHORT

Besides its height in context of the whole hand, an overlong Apollo finger can indicate that the Apollonian ideals are upside down, replacing charm and optimism with caprice and egotism. This is especially true if the three sections aren't all about the same length. An overlong tip section may mean strong creativity that isn't grounded enough in the practicalities of daily life, and this person might argue fiercely with loved ones who try to help them stabilize their lives.

LEAN IN

As with the Jupiter finger, if Saturn leans toward the Apollo finger, this means that the Apollo finger's warm joy and artful nature are mitigated or even subsumed by the pragmatism or gloominess of Saturn. If the Apollo finger leans toward a straight and tall Saturn finger, though, its charisma and optimism can help to balance any darker Saturn qualities like pessimism and melancholy. And if this person is already a strong positive Saturn, imagine what a boost of Apollo's creative energy can do!

What if the Apollo finger has a pronounced bend rather than a lean? This shows that Apollo is probably the dominant type for this person, especially if the bent finger as a whole is longer than the Jupiter finger. In turn, this type informs the rest of the features of the hand, adding a layer of artistry, aesthetics, or spontaneous creative energy.

MOUNT UP

The generally flat mount of Saturn gives way to a mount of Apollo that's often two mounts, with one that moves toward or even merges with the mount of Mercury. Remember how a strong vertical line across a mount increases its influence and magnifies that finger's trait? The common double mount of Apollo has that strong line built right in. If the Apollo mount is merged with the Mercury mount, the Apollonian qualities could express with Mercury counterparts like strategy, diplomacy, and strong work ethic.

There are only two elements that are liquids at room temperature, and the second one, bromine, wasn't discovered until the 1800s. Mercury, which constitutes less than .00001% (yes, four zeros) of Earth's crust, was discovered long enough ago that we'll never know for sure when or how it happened. Traces and samples of relatively pure mercury in liquid form have been found in containers that are at least 3,500 years old.

80

HG

MERCURY

200.59

Based on the ways mercury can be purified, it seems like ancient people probably threw beautiful rocks onto fires to see what would happen. Maybe they included the rocks in rituals or used them to decorate pyres. As the impurities burn away, mercury vapor forms and condenses into a liquid just like water does. Imagine discovering something that flows like oil but looks like a precious metal—it's not hard to see why the ancients began applying mercury to everything they could think of and valuing it in a quasi-supernatural way.

There's a major myth that Mercury is linked with medicine. This mistake is understandable, because Mercury carried a staff with two serpents wound around it, which we commonly see linked with medical offices.

But the real god of healing, Asclepius, carried a staff with just one serpent. He commanded a crew of snakes to aid in his medical work. For Mercury, the dual serpents more closely represent his changing nature and the resulting different facets of personality and behavior. His Greek equivalent Hermes had resolved a conflict between two snakes and made harmony between them, according to myth.

MERCURIAL QUICKSILVER

Because of mercury's unique nature, alchemists—the ancestors of scientists—developed a theory that the silver liquid was the "starter" that formed all solid metals. It was named hydrargyrum, "water silver," and its chemical symbol Hg comes from this name. Alchemists chose hydrargyrum as the symbolic metal for the planet Mercury. At the time, astronomers had long ago noticed that Mercury appeared and disappeared rapidly from the night sky. They'd already named the planet after the Roman messenger god.

The planets these early astronomers could see are known as the classical planets, and each has a whole series of entanglements in alchemy, astrology, and even religions of the time period. In alchemy, the major metals used during the Classical period are all tied to planets: iron for Mars, tin for Jupiter, and copper for Venus. The moon is represented by silver and the sun is represented by gold. Just one planet, Mercury, somehow impressed its name onto its metal for common usage.

Mercury is also called quicksilver, meaning "alive silver"—from the same root that led to the natal term quickening, which is when the fetus begins to feel alive within the womb. The god Mercury was lively, fast, and efficient, represented by winged sandals that enabled him to fly. Centuries later, the term light-footed emerged as a way to describe someone who is nimble and dynamic in their movements.

FINGER FEATURES

The Mercury finger is usually much shorter than the other fingers. It can seem more slender and delicate, but often it's just proportionally smaller. The Jupiter, Saturn, and Apollo fingers generally share the same level, or set, but the Mercury finger is usually set below them, which makes it look even smaller. Despite this, the top section of the Mercury finger is often the same length as the top sections of the other fingers, meaning its other two sections are where most of that missing length is.

The top section of the Mercury finger may also appear more tapered than the other fingers. A strong Mercury finger with a noticeably tapered tip can show that someone is great at communicating and doing business with people who are more powerful than themselves. They may be fine diplomats or personal assistants to finicky executives. Those with squared or flaring Mercury tips could find their strength in talking with peers to develop ideas and rapport.

JUPITER SATURN APOLLO MERCURY

STRENGTH OF WILL

GIRDLE OF VENUS

LINE OF HEART

LINE OF HEART

MARRIAGE

LOGIC

MARS

MARS

LINE OF MARS

LINE OF LIFE

LINE OF DESTINY

LINE OF SUN

LINE OF HEALTH

LINE OF INTUITION

VENUS

MOON

NEPTUNE

LONG AND SHORT

If the Mercury finger is even shorter than its usual short length, this person's communicative abilities could be limited. Mercury also represents money and business smarts, which means the short Mercury finger may find it hard to keep their own books or make big spending decisions without some support and outside resources. A straight and average or longer Mercury finger with a proportionally long top section shows the strongest communication skills.

LEAN IN

Mercury can only potentially lean toward Apollo. In that case, the more artistic Apollo will find better footing in the realm of moneymaking and administrative tasks that can stymie other creative workers. If the Apollo finger shows someone who is already industrious and dedicated to their creative career, a leaning Mercury finger gives even more strength to Apollo's executive functions. This person could be a great candidate to lead an arts fundraising organization or work in museum leadership.

MOUNT UP

The mount of Mercury often wraps around the side of the hand. It can be flush and smooth with the side of the hand or stick out slightly if it's very pronounced. If the Mercury mount stands out further than any of the others, this cancels out any issues with the Mercury finger's length. The Mercury mount may merge with one half of a double Apollo mount, giving the same influence as a leaning Mercury finger does.